What Every Ice Cream Dealer Should Know

What Every Ice Cream Dealer Should Know

A PRACTICAL
TREATISE ON ICE CREAM MAKING,
INCLUDING MANY FORMULAS,
RECIPES, ETC.

PRICE $2.00

Daly Bros. Manufacturing Corporation
Schenectady, N. Y.

J. B. LYON COMPANY
PRINTERS AND BINDERS
ALBANY, N. Y.

FOREWORD

Efficiency is the watchword of the authors of this book. After realizing the long-felt want for information concerning ice cream and soda fountains, etc., this company solved most of the necessary requirements in offering this modern publication to the trade.

The formulas, tests and advertising schemes gathered herewith are all practical. They have been gathered from colleges and from some of the most successful ice cream people of to-day, together with years of practical experience of the authors. The most successful business men are the ones who will read, reason and think. We sincerely hope this work which we have so carefully compiled will prove profitable, interesting and instructive to you.

WHAT EVERY ICE CREAM DEALER SHOULD KNOW

BRIEF HISTORY OF ICE CREAM

The Bible tells indirectly the people of Palestine knew and appreciated the refreshing quality of snow in time of harvest. The Jews, the ancient Greeks and Romans were all accustomed to the use of snow for cooling wines and other beverages, and it is to-day used in this way in certain parts of Spain and Turkey.

Alexander the Great is said to have been very fond of iced beverages, and it is said that one of our modern varieties, the "Macedoine," was named after the ancient Macedonian. Wines and fruit juices were cooled with ice and snow at the courts of France and Italy in very early times. When and where the first water ices were made no one can say, but it seems probable that they were brought to France from Italy by Catherine de Medici in the sixteenth century. Marco Polo is reported to have brought recipes for water ice and milk ice from Japan in the thirteenth century.

Cream ice was served at a banquet given by Charles I of England. This ice was made by a French cook named De Mirco, and it is related that the King was so pleased with the new dish that he pensioned the cook with 20 pounds a year on the condition that the latter should not make the ice for any one but the King, and should tell no one else how to make it.

English cook books, published about the middle of the eighteenth century, gave recipes for making cream ices. It readily can be seen how the making of ice cream has developed step by step from the cooling of wines and fruit juices to the freezing of similar liquids, and then to the freezing of milk and cream.

Ice cream is said to have been introduced to the city of Washington by Mrs. Alexander Hamilton, at a dinner that was attended by George Washington.

The first ice cream advertisement on record is one that appeared in the *Post Boy,* New York City, June 8, 1786. At this time ice cream sold at $1 per quart.

Jacob Fussell, so far as known, was the first man to make a wholesale business of ice cream making. He was a milk dealer in Baltimore, Md., and adopted ice cream making to utilize his surplus cream. A few years later, an ice company, becoming interested in the manufacture of ice cream, paid Fussell $500 for teaching one of their men the art of making this product.

American enterprise took up the new industry, and it developed steadily. However, it was not until 1890 that the rapid growth began. Since that date the business has been growing with increasing rapidity, aided, to some extent, by the perfection of artificial refrigeration. This provided a way for these frozen dainties to be used in the south, and made possible the great wholesale factories found in some of the large cities.

The value of the ice cream consumed in this country has reached the enormous figure of $200,000,000 per annum, and has outgrown the small secret chamber in which the manufacturer a few years ago performed his work.

The ice cream industry in general thus far has been slightly studied, and the brains and money that have been invested have worked wonders.

The making of ice cream has been regarded, at least in part, as a secret process. During the few years that ice cream has been made on a commercial scale, and even to-day, in many places, the mixing and freezing of ice cream has been carried on behind locked doors, too often in cellars. But it is the opinion of many of the large manufacturers that the time has come when secrecy is not necessary, nor even desirable. The making of ice cream in secret does not create a monopoly for the manufacture, nor does it increase the popularity of or demand for the product. On the other hand the making of ice cream in a modern, properly constructed, sanitary factory, open to the public, is a great advertisement for the manufacturer and is conducive to an increased demand for the product. Manufacturers of ice cream supplies are scattering broadcast exact directions for making the mix, freezing the cream, etc. Several dairy schools are teaching commercial ice cream making. Some large dealers are promulgating the opinion that ice cream making is a scientific process, and the more the subject is made public, is discussed and studied, the more perfect will the process become and the better will the product be. The better the product the greater the consumption of the same. An interesting feature of the industry to the average business concern is the supply buying. The dairy interests now count the cream demand for ice cream as being second in importance to butter and better than the cheese requirements. It is sure that the requirements for the ice cream this year has hit the butter business hard and has lifted the price of the latter. In some sections the butter men have been put out of business by the ice cream manufacturers.

Then, too, the ice cream business has created a great demand for ice cream machinery. The modern ice cream factory demands high grade valuable machinery. From the delicate brine freezer to the ponderous ice machine the total investment of a large ice cream factory amounts to impressive figures. Next year will see great strides in the growth of this industry.

FREEZING ICE CREAM

You can make or break the quality of ice cream in the freezing of it, for you can no more make a fine quality out of a poor mix than you can out of a good mix if not frozen properly.

The batch should go into the freezer at a temperature no higher than 34 degrees, the speed of the dasher or beater should be approximately 150 revolutions per minute and the brine temperature 12 degrees above zero; and it will take about 13 to 15 minutes to freeze a batch of 10 gallons. As it takes about 15 minutes running to finish a batch properly in most standard machines at 150 revolutions per minute the brine temperature will have to be adjusted to meet local conditions.

For instance there should be a brine circulation of 35 gallons per minute through freezer, if you have more the temperature will have to be raised or the circulation cut, or if the freezer has a crust accumulated around the inner barrel so as to hinder radiation the brine may have to be lowered. It is little things like these that defeat the efforts of the uninitiated.

Great care should be used in keeping paddles of freezers sharp and clean. Few ice cream men realize the advantages of sharp paddles, but if you will take in consideration how important this operation is you will watch them very carefully and scrape them often.

If sweet cream and milk is not aged enough before mixing and ripened enough after mixing you cannot get the necessary quantity of ice cream, they must be at least 48 hours old before mixing, and whatever more age can be given them without impairing the taste is beneficial. Strawberry and fruit creams will take one or two minutes longer to freeze to the proper consistency under the same conditions than plain vanilla.

The sweet cream and milk should be properly aged, the ingredients must be mixed in the right way, the batch must be run down to the proper temperature and ripened before going into the freezer, and the brine must be the right temperature to finish in from 14 to 16 minutes. Longer running will have a tendency to butter and spoil the texture of the ice cream, although when you are working on sweet cream that has not been properly aged you can get a better yield by raising the brine temperature or running three or four minutes with the brine shut off when the batch is about two-thirds frozen.

After the ice cream is frozen enough it takes a very short time to overfreeze it or freeze it down, and you can lose from three to four quarts in about one-half minute's time, if the brine is not turned off this will continue until the batch has lost from two and one-half gallons to three gallons in quantity. When the batch in the freezer has about reached the consistency of apple butter shut off the brine, after a few trials you can determine the time exactly, but do not run too long or you will lose in quantity before the freezer will empty. And as soon as the ice cream reaches the point where it commences to go down it grains and deteriorates.

Cause of Shrinking. The ice cream will not commence to go down until it becomes too hard and the freezer may run half a day if the batch is not allowed to freeze up, but if the stock is properly allowed to age before mixing, after the freezer has run about 16 minutes, buttering will commence, and as soon as it reaches this point the batch begins to separate and water out and then you have rough ice cream, although the fresher the stock before mixing the longer you can run the freezer to get the yield, but no way you can handle it can you produce as good a yield from fresh stock as you can from that which has been properly aged.

Refreezing Ice Cream. The taking back of melted ice cream as a practice should be most emphatically discouraged, because of the dangers which arise from the possible decomposition of the product and consequent ptomaine poisoning and from the danger of scattering contagious diseases. However, ice cream that for any reason has happened to melt while still new and fresh enough so that there is no danger of decomposition having started, may be refrozen by again placing it in the freezer and treating it as an ordinary run. This second freezing, however, requires a considerably longer time than does the initial effort, because of the air it contains; and, moreover, it is liable so to increase the amount of air in the cream as to cause it to become fluffy and weak bodied. Such thawed ice cream, if not old, may be mixed with the ordinary new "mix" and run out therewith without likelihood of this difficulty.

Rehardening Ice Cream. Ice cream that is being held and which has become weak from rising temperature should be rehardened with great care; for if the mass has become materially melted and then is rehardened without being run through the freezer, large water crystals will form, causing the mass to become coarse, spiny and very unpleasant. Then, again, there is a great probability that some of the skim milk portion containing large quantities of sugar has settled to the bottom, and that the portions richer in fat have moved upwards; in which case the bottom few inches of contents will be found when it reaches the consumer, to be but a little better than a lot of sweetened crystals. The mass of rehardening ice cream may be well mixed with a heavy spoon while being frozen. This procedure prevents this settling out. However, at best such rehardened ice cream will become relatively coarse grained and spiny, and a considerable loss in volume will occur.

Transferring. So far as possible all transferring and handling of the finished product should be done while it is still in a fresh condition, for it can then be managed easily and without loss, while if packed away and hardened and, later, redished into the pint, quart and gallon containers, a loss of volume results. From six to six and one-half gallons of "mix," making 10 gallons of finished ice cream

will fill 10 gallons of orders if handled while fresh, but it
will fill only nine and one-half gallons of orders if dished
24 hours later. Taking all things into account a loss of
about 10 per cent. must be expected if ice cream is moulded
or packed into small containers after it has once been
allowed to set.

ICE CREAM FILLERS

One of the fillers most widely used is called gelatine.
This substance is prepared for use by dissolving in hot
milk or water and stirring quickly into the cream. Many
experienced dealers claim that the higher priced gelatine
is cheaper in the end than the low priced goods. The
manufacturer should carefully select the gelatine in order
to be sure that it is perfectly sanitary.

At the present time gelatine is being replaced by gum
tragacanth and many other India gums. One reason for
this change is that many people and some health officers
object to the use of gelatine. They claim that it may be
dangerous to health, because it may come from diseased
animals, or it may have been contaminated before or
during the manufacturing process.

Tragacanth is a gummy exudation from plants belong-
ing to the genus Astragalus, family Leguminose. The
gum is in ribbon-shaped bands, one to three mm. thick,
long and linear, straight or spirally twisted. Tragacanth
is generally milled to a very fine powder when it is to be
used in ice cream.

" India Gum " has its origin in other plants and is
usually found in lumps, never in ribbon-shaped bands.

Modern Mixing Machines.

Because of this difference in physical characteristics adulteration of tragacanth with the cheaper gum is not attempted. But large quantities of gum are sold in the pulverized form in which no physical difference can be detected. India gums are used extensively in ice cream preparations; generally rice flour, starch or sugar is added and placed in packages and is sold for about 30 cents per pound.

Powdered arrow root, sago, iceland moss, glycerine, etc., are occasionally used in ice cream making, but have very little commercial importance.

Ice cream that is to be used in soda water must contain sufficient binder to prevent it from being broken up and dissolved by the jet of soda. Cream is often made special for fountain trade with less butter fat and more gum or gelatine.

Many ice cream men are now using glucose as a filler in addition to their gelatine or powder. They claim it helps considerable in producing a smooth ice cream. Glucose costs in the neighborhood of three cents per pound and it adds the bulk of the cream.

There are several advantages in using a good strong ice cream powder, but the only drawback has been the wasteful method of mixing with sugar. However, this has been overcome by a mixing machine which is now on the market. These machines are inclosed so as to prevent the powder from flying around the mixing room. They are now in practical operation by many of the larger dealers successfully. They are a great time saver for the ice cream maker. These machines perform two operations, that is to say they make ice cream powder and also mix it for the batch.

Many of the dealers are making their own ice cream powder, simply by reducing the strongest kinds of powdered gums, such as tragacanth and many others which mostly are imported.

By reducing these strong powdered gums with powdered sugar or flour it has a tendency to dissolve quicker and better in the cream. A good grade of ice cream powder can be made at an approximate cost of 14 cents per pound, simply by mixing very thoroughly one part of powdered gum tragacanth or India gum with about four parts of powdered sugar or flour.

EFFECTS OF GELATINE IN ICE CREAM

Gelatine does not increase the swell, gums may or do assist some in getting and retaining a swell, because they retain their viscosity until actually frozen. Sugar is probably more important in this respect than either gelatine or vegetable gums, as it is very tenacious in the syrupy form and increases in viscosity as the temperature lowers until frozen, freezing at a temperature of 28 degrees Fahrenheit.

The best results in the use of gelatine, tragacanth and other gums were obtained with the moderate use of each. The tragacanth or other vegetable gums are to be used in a powdered form, not pure, but mixed with powdered sugar, 'rice flour, or some other powdered article of this nature. To add gum in the form of a liquid having first dissolved it in water is to add a very appreciable amount of water to the mix. If, however, it is added in the powder form it will dissolve or absorb a considerable amount of water

DALY ICE CREAM POWDER AND SUGAR MIXING MACHINE.

2

in the cream, thus causing the product to be drier than would be the case if no absorber were added. Thus we find the gum doing twofold work; that of holding the mass intact and at the same time drying it.

The function of gelatine in ice cream is to form a capsule or leather-like coating around the minute water crystals and thus prevent them from growing into sharp needles as quickly as if nothing were added to prevent this. This view is supported by the fact that gelatine is a liquid when hot, but solid when cold. The moment the gelatine is mixed with cold cream and is lowered in temperature to the neighborhood of 40 degrees it hardens, ceases to be viscid, becomes brittle and breaks apart when agitated and would release any air bubbles held by it.

The use of gelatine, tragacanth or some other like vegetable gum is practically necessary in the manufacture of commercial ice cream.

The use of these fillers, binders and smootheners does not increase the amount of swell in the finished product.

The use of a small amount of gum tragacanth or India gums with a small amount of gelatine produces the best results. In this ice cream the chance of crystallization is eliminated and the benefit of a smoothener is obtained.

The amount of fat in the cream has but little effect on the amount of air that can be whipped into the mix, but has much to do with the amount which will remain incorporated.

The age of the cream may add to the amount of air that will be retained in the finished product, as age adds to the viscosity of cream and so adds to the retaining power,

HOW TO DISSOLVE GELATINE SUCCESSFULLY

There are several grades of gelatine and it is essential to use one that does not have a rank gluey taste and smell. Many experienced ice cream makers claim that the higher grades of gelatine are cheaper in the long run to use than the cheaper grades.

Fine granulated gelatine is the best to use, on account of the ease by which it can be dissolved. However, there are many ice cream dealers using gelatine in the flake form with satisfaction.

Gelatine is generally used in quantities of about three to five ounces to each 10 gallon batch of ice cream. To dissolve gelatine place the required quantity into a small portion of water. One quart of water is sufficient for each batch. Place into a double kettle and heat up to about 150 degrees or enough to dissolve it very thoroughly, then strain. Place this dissolved gelatine into a small portion of the ice cream mix, not to exceed two quarts to this small portion of gelatine, then mix well for a short time and place it into the remainder of the ice cream mixture and it will be ready to freeze.

Another simple way of dissolving gelatine is to mix the same proportions into about one quart of boiling water, then strain and add about two quarts of the ice cream mixture or milk. Mix thoroughly and add it to the remainder of the batch and freeze.

It is not necessary to have a steam jacket kettle or a double boiler for this kind of work, although they come in play if you don't have boiling water.

INFLUENCE OF GELATIN, GUM TRAGACANTH AND ICE CREAM POW. DERS ON OVERRUN, BODY AND TEXTURE.

Filler used	Brine temperature	Time to freeze	Overrun	Body and texture
	Deg. F.	Min.	Per ct.	
None..............	8-10	13	65	Firm, little icy in 24 hours.
Gelatin..............	8-10	13	66	Firm, no ice crystals.
None..............	8-10	12	58	Icy in 24 hours.
Gum, trag. and gelatin	8-10	13	59	Smooth, firm, no ice crystals.
Mellowine powder....	12-14	17	50	Smooth, occasional ice crystals.
Purity powder........	12-14	18	52	Smooth, firm, occasional ice crystals in 24 hours.
None..............	18-20	20	55	Icy, coarse.
Gum tragacanth......	18-20	21	55	Smooth, little icy in 24 hours.
Gum trag. and gelatin	18-20	22	57	Firm, smooth, no crystals.
Gelatin..............	18-20	13	55	No ice crystals, not smooth.
Gelatin..............	18-20	19	58	No ice crystals, not smooth.
Gelatin...........	14-16	19	53	Smooth, no ice crystals.
None..............	8-10	14	54	In all three freezings.
None..............	18-20	19	57	Ice crystals were present in 24 hours.
Purity powder........ {	14-16 / 14-16	15 / 14	52 / 55	} Smooth, few ice crystals.
Mellowine powder....	14-16	15	54	Smooth, few ice crystals.
Gum trag. and gelatin {	18-20 / 10-12 / 14-16	20 / 12 / 14	60 / 48 / 50	} Good, smooth, firm body, no ice crystals.
None.............. {	18-20 / 18-20 / 18-20	19 / 18 / 19	60 / 58 / 61	} Icy and coarse.

COMMERCIAL ICE CREAM FORMULAS

Ice cream formulas can be obtained in numerous quantities, but the main object is to please the majority of the public, and still realize a fair profit, so we have selected the following formulas from several of the largest and most successful ice cream manufacturers in the world.

It is now up to you to select or make your choice of the recipes suitable for the class of trade you have, taking in consideration the price you are going to ask for your products. However, we suggest that you consider quality first, as experience has proven that it pays in the long run to use at least a fair grade of cream.

In order to simplify these formulas we are using vanilla ice cream chiefly, as this flavor is the best seller and contains approximately the same proportions of cream, sugar, etc., as most other flavors do.

Vanilla ice cream is especially accommodating, in that though of itself it is one of the most popular of flavors, its flavor is yet so delicate that it easily gives way to other stronger ones, like chocolate or coffee; so that if but a single quart or gallon of coffee ice cream is ordered, it is not infrequent practice in the trade to mix a small quantity of the flavor with a sufficient quantity of vanilla ice cream, and thus to accommodate the consumer and relieve the dealer of certain embarrassments. Or if, say, vanilla, coffee and strawberry ice creams are desired, the stock for the entire three kinds are made up as one batch, then used first as vanilla to the extent desired, then as coffee, and then as strawberry, one after the other, all from one and the same vanilla mix without washing the machine, and usually to the entire satisfaction of all concerned.

Vanilla flavor is necessary in most all flavors of ice cream, as it has a tendency to prevent any unpleasant aftertastes that may occur.

MODIFICATION TABLE FOR USE IN MAKING APPROXIMATELY TEN GALLONS OF ICE CREAM.

Showing the approximate amounts of cream and of skimmilk needed to obtain 6 gallons of cream before freezing. The figures are stated as GALLONS.

Quality desired	10%	12%	15%	18%	20%	22%	25%
+ind of stock:							
18% cream,	3 1/3	4	5	6	.....	.....	......
Skimmilk,	2 2/3	2	1	0	.....	.....	......
20% cream,	3	4	4 1/2	5 1/3	6	.....	......
Skimmilk,	3	2	1 1/2	2/3	0	.....	......
22% cream,	2 2/3	3 1/3	4	5	5 1/2	6	......
Skimmilk,	3 1/3	2 2/3	2	1	1/2	0	......
25% cream,	2 2/5	3	3 3/5	4 1/3	4 4/5	5 1/3	6
Skimmilk,	3 3/5	3+	2 2/5	1 2/3	1 1/5	2/3	0
30% cream,	2	2 1/2—	3	3 3/5	4	4 1/3	5
Skimmilk,	4	3 1/2+	3	2 2/5	2	1 2/3	1
35% cream,	2—	2+	2 2/3	3+	3 3/7	3 3/4	4 2/7
Skimmilk,	4+	4—	3 1/3	3—	2 4/7	2 1/4	1 5/7
40% cream,	1 1/2	1 4/5	2 1/4	2 3/4	3	3 3/10	3 3/4
Skimmilk.	4 1/2	4 1/5	3 3/4	3 1/4	3	2 3/10	2 1/4

NOTE.—This table may be used as follows: An 18% cream is to be frozen. One has a 30% cream on hand and skimmilk. One follows the perpendicular column headed 18% downwards until the location is reached which is on the horizontal line bearing the title at the left "30% cream." The figures at this point show the proportions of 30% cream (3⅗ gallons) and of skimmilk (2⅖ gallons) needed to make an 18% cream.

STANDARD VANILLA ICE CREAM No. 1

The following is a formula especially good for a high class retail trade:

20 quarts 18 per cent. cream.
8 pounds granulated sugar.
4 ounces vanilla extract.
4 ounces gelatine or a strong powdered gum.

STANDARD VANILLA ICE CREAM No. 2

16 quarts 20 per cent. cream.
4 quarts condensed milk.
7 pounds granulated sugar.
3 ounces vanilla extract.
4 ounces gelatine.

STANDARD VANILLA ICE CREAM No. 3

This formula does not have sufficient percentage of fat to be called ice cream. However, some dealers are using it to some extent, they call it picnic ice cream. It is generally sold to places of amusement where repeat orders are not expected. We do not recommend the use of it.

14 quarts of condensed milk.
10 quarts fresh milk.
8 pounds sugar.
8 ounces gelatine.
4 ounces vanilla extract.

STANDARD VANILLA ICE CREAM No. 4

11 quarts of 40 per cent. cream.
9 quarts skimmilk.
8 pounds sugar.
4 ounces vanilla extract.
3 ounces gelatine.
1 ounce powdered India gum.

STANDARD VANILLA ICE CREAM No. 5

16 quarts homogenized cream, 12 per cent.

4 quarts unsweetened condensed milk.

4 ounces vanilla extract.

8 pounds of sugar.

4 ounces gelatine.

1 ounce of tragacanth or India gum.

1 quart glucose after being dissolved by heating.

STANDARD VANILLA ICE CREAM No. 6

18 quarts homogenized cream, 12 per cent.

2 quarts condensed milk, unsweetened.

8 pounds sugar.

2 to 4 ounces vanilla extract.

3 ounces gelatine.

1 ounce of India gum, powdered.

STANDARD VANILLA ICE CREAM No. 7

16 quarts homogenized cream, 12 per cent.

4 quarts heavy cream, 40 per cent.

8 pounds granulated sugar.

10 ounces of any high grade ice cream powder.

3 ounces vanilla extract.

STANDARD VANILLA ICE CREAM No. 8

16 quarts 20 per cent. cream.

4 quarts milk.

4 quarts condensed milk, unsweetened.

4 ounces gelatine.

8 pounds granulated sugar.

4 ounces vanilla extract.

STANDARD VANILLA ICE CREAM No. 9

9 quarts 40 per cent. cream.

9 quarts skimmilk.

2 quarts unsweetened condensed milk.

3 to 4 ounces vanilla extract.

4 ounces gelatine.

1 ounce powdered India gum.

8 pounds sugar.

STANDARD VANILLA ICE CREAM No. 10

11 quarts 30 per cent. cream.

4 quarts unsweetened condensed milk.

5 quarts skimmilk.

8 pounds sugar.

4 ounces gelatine or a strong powdered gum.

4 ounces vanilla extract.

STANDARD VANILLA ICE CREAM No. 11

10 quarts of 40 per cent. cream.

10 quarts skimmilk.

8½ pounds sugar.

3 to 4 ounces vanilla extract.

1 quart dissolved glucose.

8 ounces Jersey ice cream powder.

STANDARD VANILLA ICE CREAM No. 12

8 quarts 40 per cent. cream.

4 quarts unsweetened condensed milk.

8 quarts skimmilk.

7½ pounds sugar.

3 to 4 ounces vanilla extract.

2 ounces of tragacanth or powdered India gum.

STANDARD VANILLA ICE CREAM No. 13

7 quarts heavy 40 per cent. cream.

11 quarts milk.

2 quarts condensed milk unsweetened.

4 ounces vanilla extract.

4 ounces gelatine or about 10 ounces of prepared ice cream powder.

8 pounds of granulated sugar.

STANDARD VANILLA ICE CREAM No. 14

6 quarts of heavy cream about 40 per cent.

10 quarts of milk.

4 quarts of condensed milk, unsweetened.

2 ounces gelatine.

2 ounces tragacanth or any other strong India gum.

7½ pounds of granulated sugar.

Vanilla extract, use in proportion to strength.

STANDARD VANILLA ICE CREAM No. 15

5 quarts heavy cream.

11 quarts milk.

4 quarts condensed milk, unsweetened.

8½ pounds granulated sugar.

Vanilla extract, about 3 ounces.

1 quart glucose, dissolve by heating.

10 ounces ice cream powder or 3 ounces gelatine.

STANDARD VANILLA ICE CREAM No. 16

9 quarts heavy cream.

11 quarts milk.

9 pounds sugar.

5 ounces gelatine.

1 ounce India gum (powdered).

Vanilla extract, 2 to 5 ounces.

STRAWBERRY ICE CREAM

In making strawberry ice cream use any of the standard 10-gallon formulas for vanilla ice cream, to which add 1½ quarts of crushed fresh strawberries if possible. If fresh berries are not on hand use about 3 quarts of the best obtainable. Color slightly with red coloring. Some dealers use as high as 4 quarts of berries to this size batch. Freeze the same as other flavors.

CARAMEL ICE CREAM

Caramel ice cream is becoming very popular in some states and is simply made by adding about 6 to 10 ounces to a 10-gallon batch of ice cream. Many dealers use a prepared extract called caramala which seems to give good results.

MAPLE NUT ICE CREAM

Maple nut ice cream is a good selling ice cream and is made by adding 1 ounce maple extract and about 1 pound walnut meats crushed. Add these to the standard formula which you select.

COFFEE ICE CREAM

Use any of the standard 10-gallon batches and add 12 ounces of the best coffee extract you can obtain. Or if fresh coffee is preferred take 1 pound or 1½ pounds of good coffee, boil and strain into the batch and it will be ready to freeze.

TUTTI FRUTTI ICE CREAM

Select a standard formula for 10-gallon batch and add 2 quarts of prepared tutti frutti which is made for soda fountain use. Pour into cream and color with a very small quantity of strawberry coloring. The name tutti frutti means " all fruits." In preference to using this kind of prepared fruit some dealers use 1 pound of maraschino cherries and 2 pounds of assorted glaced fruit after cutting them in small pieces and soaking in a quart of brandy for a few hours. A small portion of cinnamon will give it a fine flavor.

PEACH ICE CREAM

To any standard 10-gallon batch, add about 3 quarts of canned peaches, or if fresh ones are in season then mash them up to a pulp. Most ice cream makers use a little orange coloring.

MAPLE ICE CREAM

Use any of the standard formulas to which add about 1 to 2 ounces of maple extract and it will be ready to freeze. Maple extracts vary considerable in strength and quality. Good judgment is required. Freeze in usual way.

LEMON ICE CREAM

Take any mix for a 10-gallon batch to which add 1 ounce of lemon emulsion. Emulsions of this kind should be mixed with a small portion of granulated sugar before placing into the mixture of cream. Many dealers are using lemon extract in making this kind of ice cream, using in proportion to its strength from 5 to 10 ounces to a batch of 10 gallons. Freeze the same as other flavors.

CHOCOLATE ICE CREAM

Select a favorable standard 10-gallon batch, to which add a high grade of cocoa in quantities of 1 pound to 1½ pounds per batch. Before placing the cocoa into the mix, take about

1 pound to which mix into 1 pound of granulated sugar, then dissolve in boiling water. After doing this it is ready to put in the 10-gallon mix. A pinch of salt will help bring the flavor. Use 2 ounces vanilla.

Many dealers use bitter chocolate which appears to be serviceable in a wholesale way. For a 10-gallon batch of ice cream, about 1 quart of a chocolate stock may be used, made essentially as follows: 1½ quarts of water, 2 pounds of bitter chocolate, shaved fine, and 4 pounds of sugar. The chocolate is put into a pan and a little water added. The mass is slowly heated, worked into a paste, more water is then added and the working continued until the mass is smooth. Half the sugar is then added; the mass heated and again it is worked smooth. Then the remaining water is added, the mixture brought nearly to a boil and the remaining sugar added. It is then stirred and brought to a boil, care being taken not to allow it to scorch. The finished product is then poured into fruit jars for future use. In addition to the chocolate flavor, about 3 ounces of vanilla extract, and if desired, ½ ounce of cinnamon extract may be used. The color will need be deepened for some trades by the addition of from 1 to 1½ ounces of caramel.

PINEAPPLE ICE CREAM

To any of the standard vanilla mixes, add about 2 quarts of crushed pineapple fruit. Add a small portion of lemon color and freeze.

BANANA ICE CREAM

To any of the standard 10-gallon vanilla batches, add one dozen good ripe bananas crushed and freeze.

CHERRY ICE CREAM

Select any of the standard vanilla batches to which add about 2 or 3 quarts of crushed cherries. Use a small amount of red color and it is ready to freeze.

ORANGE ICE CREAM

Select a standard vanilla extract for a 10-gallon batch, to which add about 1 ounce of orange emulsion. Emulsions of this kind should be mixed with a small portion of sugar before mixing in batch.

Many dealers are using orange extract in making this kind of ice cream, using in proportion to the strength of the extract. It generally requires about 5 to 10 ounces to a 10-gallon mix. Freeze as usually.

ALMOND ICE CREAM

Select a standard vanilla batch, and then add about 5 ounces of extract of almond and about 1 pound of finely crushed almonds. Freeze the same as other flavors.

PISTACHIO ICE CREAM

Select a 10-gallon standard vanilla batch, to which add 1 pound of pistachio nuts and about 2 or 3 ounces of pistachio extract. Some ice cream makers use almond extract in preference to pistachio. Use a small portion of green color. Freeze in usual way.

SHERRY ICE CREAM.

In making sherry ice cream take a quantity of fresh frozen vanilla cream and mix into it 1 quart of sherry wine to each gallon.

BISQUE ICE CREAM.

Bisque ice cream is one made from a plain vanilla mix, by mixing into it a portion of baker's products, such as sponge cake, macaroons and in many cases plain grape nut is used. While others are using almond paste. All of the above articles are used in quantities of various amounts. One pound to each gallon of ice cream works well. In all cases the cake, grape nuts or other articles should be crisp.

RASPBERRY ICE CREAM.

Select a standard mix and add to it approximately 2 quarts of raspberries to each 10-gallon batch. Freeze in usual way.

FRENCH VANILLA ICE CREAM

6 quarts 14 per cent. cream.
24 whole eggs.
4 pounds granulated sugar.
1½ ounces vanilla extract.

3

FRENCH VANILLA ICE CREAM No. 2

3 quarts 20 per cent. cream.

3 quarts milk.

2½ pounds sugar.

18 egg yolks.

Vanilla extract. Use in proportion to strength.

FRENCH VANILLA ICE CREAM No. 3

6 quarts 20 per cent. cream.

24 whole eggs.

3½ pounds sugar.

1 ounce vanilla extract.

Do not allow too great a swell in making French ice cream.

SHERBETS AND WATER ICES

Sherbets are classified as a frozen product made from water and flavored with fruit juices or other natural flavors generally containing eggs or a portion of milk or condensed milk.

Ices are very similar to sherbets excepting that they are made without the use of eggs or milk. Ices and sherbets are froze in the same manner as ice cream.

PINEAPPLE ICE

10 quarts of water.

10 pounds of sugar.

2 quarts of crushed pineapple.

Citric acid solution, sufficient to give tart.

TUTTI-FRUTTI ICE

10 quarts of water.

10 pounds of sugar.

2 quarts of prepared tutti frutti.

Citric acid to obtain sufficient tart.

GRAPE ICE

10 quarts of water.

10 pounds of sugar.

2 or 3 quarts of grape juice.

Citric acid, about 4 ounces.

CHERRY ICE

10 quarts water.

10 pounds sugar.

2 or 3 quarts of crushed cherries.

4 ounces of citric acid solution.

ORANGE ICE

10 quarts water.

10 pounds granulated sugar.

1 ounce orange emulsion.

Fruit acid solution (citric acid), use in proportion to strength, 2 to 5 ounces may be used.

ORANGE ICE

6 gallons of water.
6 quarts of orange juice.
23 pounds sugar.
2 ounces gelatine.
1 pint lemon juice.

———

STRAWBERRY ICE

10 quarts of water.
10 pounds of sugar.
4 quarts fresh strawberries.
Juice of 10 lemons, or about 4 ounces citric acid.

———

FROZEN STRAWBERRIES

Use about 12 quarts of fresh strawberries to which add 12 quarts of water, 10 pounds of granulated sugar and 4 ounces of citric acid solution. Freeze the same as water ices.

———

RASPBERRY ICE

10 quarts water.
10 pounds sugar.
2 quarts raspberries.
Fruit acid solution to give sufficient tart.

———

ORANGE SHERBET

The following is a formula intended for a high class retail trade and is seldom used for wholesale purposes:
6 gallons water or milk.
6 quarts orange juice.

1 pint lemon juice.

2 dozen eggs, whites only.

23 pounds sugar.

STRAWBERRY SHERBET

Another recipe for a very delicious sherbet is as follows:

1 quart of water.

1 pound of sugar.

1 quart strawberries.

Whites of 6 eggs.

Juice of 2 lemons.

ORANGE OR LEMON SHERBET

This formula is used by several wholesale ice cream factories with success:

10 quarts water.

10 pounds sugar.

5 quarts condensed milk.

1 ounce orange or lemon emulsion.

Fruit acid solution, use in proportion to strength, or sufficient to give a good tart.

RASPBERRY SHERBET

10 quarts water.

10 pounds sugar.

2 quarts raspberries.

5 quarts condensed milk, unsweetened.

Sufficient fruit acid to give a good tart.

GRAPE PUNCH

10 quarts water.

2 pounds sugar.

2 quarts grape juice.

1 ounce orange emulsion.

5 ounces citric acid solution, or you may use in proportion to strength of acid.

ORANGE PUNCH

10 quarts water.

2½ pounds granulated sugar.

1 ounce orange emulsion.

Citric acid to obtain sufficient tart.

Orange color.

Sliced oranges may be added if desired.

LEMON PUNCH

10 quarts water.

2½ pounds sugar.

1 ounce lemon emulsion.

Citric acid, sufficient to obtain tart.

Lemon color.

Sliced lemons if desired.

FRUIT PUNCH

10 quarts water.

2 pounds granulated sugar.

1 quart cherry syrup.

4 ounces citric acid.

1 quart maraschino cherries.

1 ounce extract almond.

Sliced oranges and lemons are generally added.

Color dark red.

———

CHERRY PUNCH

10 quarts water.

2½ pounds sugar.

2 quarts cherry syrup.

2 ounces extract almond.

Color if desired.

———

FROZEN PUNCHES

Frozen punches are made in endless variety and most dealers take orange or lemon ice and mix into them a quantity of liquors, such as Jamaica rum, maraschino cherries, brandy, wine, etc. Most ice cream makers use their own original idea in selecting the quality and quantity of additional fruits, etc., taking in consideration the selling price of the product.

———

ROMAN PUNCH No. 1

Take 1 gallon of orange or lemon ice and mix with this quantity about 1 pint of Jamaica rum. This is to be colored dark red.

———

ROMAN PUNCH No. 2

Four quarts water, 4 pounds of sugar, juice of 12 lemons, small portion of red color. Freeze as you do water ice and when nearly frozen mix in about 1 pint of the Santa Cruz rum.

___

FROZEN CLARET PUNCH

4 quarts water ice.
1 quart claret wine.
Color dark red if necessary.
Mix well and pack in salt and ice.

___

FROZEN MARASCHINO PUNCH

4 quarts water ice.
1½ pint maraschino.
1 pint brandy.
1 pint maraschino cherries.
Mix very thoroughly and pack in salt and ice.

___

FROZEN KIRSCHENWASSER PUNCH

4 quarts of water ice.
1 pint Kiscjenwasser.
1 pint brandy.
Mix thoroughly and pack.

___

FROZEN FRUIT PUNCH

1 gallon water ice.
1 pint maraschino cherries.
1 pint crushed pineapple.
1 pint strawberries.

KNICKERBOCKER PUNCH, FROZEN

1 gallon water ice.
1 pint brandy.
1 pint sherry wine.
1 pint maraschino cherries.
Mix very thoroughly and then pack in salt and ice.
Color red.

————

CREME DE MENTHE FROZEN PUNCH

1 gallon water ice.
1 pint creme de menthe.
1 pint brandy.
· Green color.
1 pint maraschino cherries.
Mix well and then pack in salt and ice.

————

ORANGES FILLED WITH FROZEN PUNCH

Select oranges of a medium size and cut out a round piece off the top about the size of a quarter. Do not cut off entirely as this round piece may act as a lid. Remove the contents of the orange as much as possible, pliers does this in a fine shape. After you have removed the inside of the oranges, then rinse off in cold water. Fill them with any kind of frozen punch, sherbet or water ice. As each orange is filled, then replace the lid or the top of the orange, then tie a half-inch silk ribbon around the oranges which will hold the lid on.

Pack in brick ice cream cans, those with shelves are preferable. Serve on doilies.

SULTANA ROLL

In making sultana rolls there is a round mould that is made for this purpose. The mould is generally lined with pistachio ice cream and the center filled with tutti frutti ice cream. Some dealers simply line the mould with chocolate ice cream and fill the center with vanilla ice cream, into which they mix about ½ pound of sultana raisins, after they have been soaked in brandy.

NESSELRODE PUDDING

There are several ways of making nesselrode puddings, and it is generally left to the good judgment of the maker. That is to say very few frozen puddings are made alike. They are simply an ice cream very highly flavored, with a generous amount of fruit, raisins, and generally a small portion of brandy is added. They are most always packed in melon moulds or brick moulds. Sauces are made special for frozen puddings. Some firms are using the following mixture with success:

1 gallon fresh made ice cream.
1 pint rum.
1 pint maraschino cherries cut in small pieces.
1 pound marroons.
½ pound sultana raisins.

MONTROSE PUDDING

Take a two quart melon or a brick mould, then place into it a layer of vanilla ice cream, then a layer of cut glaced fruit on top of this layer place still another layer of vanilla ice cream and so on until the mould is completed. Close the mould and pack in salt and ice for about two hours.

MOUSSES

Mousses are made from whipped cream, partly frozen to which sugar, fruits, juices, other flavors, or nuts have been added. They are generally placed in melon moulds and served in paper cases.

ORANGE MOUSSE

Whip 1 quart of heavy cream to a stiff froth, add 1 pound of sugar dissolved in 1 pint of orange juice. Place in mould and pack with salt and ice for about 2 hours. Serve in paper cases.

STRAWBERRY MOUSSE

Whip up about 1 quart of heavy cream to a stiff froth, to which add 1 quart of fresh crushed strawberries and ½ pound powdered sugar. Pack in melon mould for approximately two hours. Serve in paper cases.

MARASCHINO MOUSSE

Whip up 1 quart of heavy cream, to which add about 6 ounces of sugar, ½ pint maraschino cherries and ½ pint cherry juice. Pack in mould to freeze to a semi consistency brick ice cream.

CLARET MOUSSE

Whip up 1 quart of heavy cream, after which add about ½ pint of claret wine and 6 ounces of sugar. Pack in melon mould.

PEACH MOUSSE

Whip up 1 quart of heavy cream, after which add about 1 pint of peach juice and about 6 ounces sugar. Pack in mould to harden. Serve in paper cases.

SHERRY MOUSSE

Whip up 1 quart of heavy cream, after which add about ½ pint of sherry wine and about 6 ounces of sugar. Pack in melon mould.

PROPER BLENDING OF SALT AND ICE IN PACKING ICE CREAM

In packing ice cream with salt and ice, most dealers use ground rock salt in preference to fine salt because the former can be mixed more uniformly through the crushed ice, and does not dissolve too rapidly. Fine salt dissolves almost immediately, causes pieces of ice to freeze together into chunks, and does not form so uniform a freezing mixture as does the crushed rock salt.

One part of salt mixed with about twelve parts of ice will freeze the cream and keep it hard the proper amount of

time. But the amount must be varied to suit conditions.
The maker needs to use judgment in this respect.

Ice and salt are sometimes mixed on the floor in a manner similar to that of mixing feed, but this practice has
two objectionable features; first, a great deal of the ice
will melt before it can be used, thus causing a needless
waste of ice; and, secondly, just as great a quantity of salt
will be put into the bottom of the tub as on the top, thus
causing a needless waste of salt.

There is little or no necessity for putting salt into the
bottom of the tub, because the salt above is being washed
down by the melted ice. No salt need be added until the
packing tub has been half filled with ice. At this point a
portion of the salt should be added, and then relatively
greater portions added as the tub is filled. Crushed ice,
free from salt, may be first added, then the mixture of
crushed ice and salt. In this manner the salt and ice may
be mixed in a box or on the floor.

In the winter, when the freezing is done in a cold room,
it is sometimes noticed that an unusually long time is required to freeze the cream. This is undoubtedly due to the
surrounding temperature retarding the melting of the ice.
When the melting is delayed, the absorption of heat from the
cream is delayed and, therefore, the freezing process
is retarded. In the cold room the ice around the freezers
does not melt and form brine rapidly; hence, heat can be
conducted from the cream only at points where the ice particles are against the can, and this is but a relatively small
proportion of the entire surface of the freezing can, and
hence conducts the heat from the cream more rapidly. To
overcome this slow formation of brine, it is recommended
that some water be poured over the ice and salt mixture.

COMPOSITION OF MILK

Probably no other food found in nature, except meat, is subject to such great variation in composition as in milk. The average composition of American milk, according to Babcock, is:

Water 87.17
Fat 3.69
Casein 3.02
Albumen 53
Sugar 4.88
Ash 71

The milk of individual animals varies from day to day, and varies as the period of lactation advances. However, the mixed milk from a large herd is not subject to very great variations, but the milk of one herd may differ greatly from that of another herd, due to the breed of the cattle. The constituents subject to the greatest variation are the fat and casein. The following table shows this:

Breed	Per cent fat	Per cent casein	Per cent total solids
Holstein	3.26	2.20	11.80
Ayrshire	3.76	2.46	12.75
Shorthorn	4.28	2.79	14.30
Devon	4.89	3.10	14.50
Guernsey	5.38	2.91	14.90
Jersey	5.78	3.03	15.40

Milk from one dealer may contain 25 per cent. to 40 per cent. more nutrients than milk from another dealer, but in the same locality the consumer usually pays the same price for both.

BACTERIA IN ICE CREAM

The subject of bacteria in ice cream has received attention only during the past few years. There is a popular belief that, because cream is frozen, it cannot decompose and that the organisms originally in the cream are killed or rendered harmless by the continued low temperature. However, experiments show that bacteria do remain virile and that certain types even proliferate at subfreezing temperatures. The bacterial content of ice cream, then, is a matter of importance from a hygienic standpoint.

We have previously noted that the conditions of the milk and cream supply in many localities are far from ideal. Since milk and cream are the main constituents of ice cream, this later product cannot be of any better quality than the materials of which it is made. However, all the methods of improving milk and cream are just as applicable to the ice cream industry as to city milk supply.

Investigations of conditions in Washington, D. C., reported in Bulletin 56 of the Hygienic Laboratory, show that, in 130 samples of cream examined, the average number of bacteria per cubic centimeter was 12,130,080. At the same time 381 samples of milk were subjected to a bacteriological examination and the average number of organisms per cubic centimeter was 3,415,533. Samples of ice cream at the same time contained from 100,000 to 400,000,000 bacteria per cubic centimeter.

Dr. George W. Stiles of Washington, D. C., investigated the bacterial flora of ice cream in cold storage, and secured the following results:

Four samples of ice cream were secured from different dealers and placed in storage at a temperature varying from 0° to 0° F. The bacterial content of these samples averaged on the

	Per c. c.
Initial count..............................	70,000,000
3d day........................	120,000,000
6th day........................	65,000,000
9th day........................	80,000,000
11th day........................	50,000,000
14th day........................	13,000,000
17th day........................	21,000,000
20th day........................	85,000,000
23d day........................	90,000,000
27th day........................	225,000,000
30th day........................	22,000,000
34th day........................	13,000,000

Just what significance should be attached to these bacterial counts depends chiefly upon the types of kinds of organisms that are present in the ice cream. Certain varieties may produce toxins, while others are harmless.

Cases are on record where ice cream caused digestive derangements, headache, diarrhea and symptoms of poisoning soon after eating. Such cases of illness are commonly explained as ptomaine poisoning, are usually due to unsanitary conditions of the raw material (cream, gelatine, etc.), the ice cream factory, or prolonged storage of the ice cream.

The owners of one large ice cream factory guarantee their product sold to be absolutely free from tubercle bacilli, and other disease-producing bacteria, and to contain no more than 25,000 germs per cubic centimeter when delivered to the customer. At this particular plant a bacterial count is made (1) of the cream after homogenization, (2) of the mix before freezing and (3) of the frozen product ready for shipment. The counts run, on an average, about as follows: Cream, 2,000 bacteria per cubic centimeter; mix, 12,000 per cubic centimeter, and ice cream, 24,000 per cubic centimeter. The ice cream is also tested for gas-producing organisms, any bacteria of the B. Coli type being considered a very objectionable contamination. The analysis report card used in this work is as follows:

BACTERIOLOGICAL ANALYSIS OF ICE CREAM

Ice cream examined................................
No. of plates used for each dilution.................
Average number of bacteria in dilution..............1—   100..Per c. c.
Average number of bacteria in dilution..............1—   1,000..Per c. c.
Average number of bacteria in dilution..............1—   5,000..Per c. c.
Average number of bacteria in dilution..............1—   10,000..Per c. c.
Average number of bacteria in dilution..............1—100,000..Per c. c.
Gas .... per cent., Co_2 .... per cent., H_2 .... per cent., B. Coli Communis..
Date cream made............................. 19..
Date of analysis .... 19..
Date plates " counted " ....:..... 19..

Signed ....,

Bacteriologist.

BACTERIAL WORK ON ICE CREAM

The two most important factors causing a high bacterial content in ice cream are, time of ripening the cream, and the mechanical agitation during freezing.

The ingredients used in the manufacture of ice cream are also of bacteria found in ice cream. The freezer and other utensils may also add to the number of organisms present unless given proper attention. Gelatin is not heated high enough to destroy many bacteria. Very few bacteria are found in flavors as from 20 to 40 per cent. of the various flavors is alcohol, which is considered to have some germicidal properties.

4

In nearly all of the tests run on samples of ice cream held for 24 to 48 hours, no appreciable increase was noticed in the number of organisms present. In several cases a decided increase was noticed; this I believe was due to allowing the frozen product to soften up to a considerable degree, and then reharden.

BACTERIAL WORK ON IOE CREAM

Sample	Time held	Date secured	Manufacturer	Bacterial content
				Per cent
1	2 hours	2-15-13	"A"	5,000,000
2	2 hours	2-15-13	"B"	9,000,000
3	2 hours	2-16-13	"C"	3,000,000
4	2 hours	2-16-13	"D"	22,000,000
5 (1)	24 hours	2-15-13	"A"	5,800,000
6 (2)	24 hours	2-15-13	"B"	8,500,000
7 (1)	48 hours	2-15-13	"A"	6,000,000
8 (2)	48 hours	2-15-13	"B"	8,400,000
9	2 hours	2-17-13	"E"	10,000,000
10	2 hours	2-17-13	"F"	20,000,000
11	24 hours	2-17-13	"C"	3,000,000
12	24 hours	2-17-13	"D"	21,600,000
13	2 hours	2-18-13	"G"	8,000,000
14	48 hours	2-16-13	"C"	21,800,000
15	48 hours	2-16-13	"D"	21,000,000
16	2 hours	2-20-13	"A"	10,000,000
17	2 hours	2-20-13	"B"	8,000,000
18	2 hours	2-21-13	"C"	5,000,000
19	2 hours	2-21-13	"D"	30,000,000
21	2 hours	2-22-13	"A"	7,000,000
22	24 hours	2-20-13	"A"	8,000,000
23	24 hours	2-20-13	"B"	9,000,000
24	48 hours	2-20-13	"A"	10,000,000
25	48 hours	2-20-13	"B"	10,000,000
26	2 hours	2-23-13	"E"	12,000,000
27	2 hours	2-23-13	"F"	24,000,000
28	2 hours	2-24-13	"G"	9,000,000
29	24 hours	2-3-13	"E"	12,000,000
30	24 hours	2-23-13	"F"	30,000,000

In the case of samples held over the difference in the count is probably due to experimental error.

THE ICE CREAM BUSINESS AND WHAT IT HAS DONE FOR DAIRYING

Ice cream appears to be the equalizer and shock absorber of our dairy industry, and a sort of market representative for the cow, says the *Country Gentleman*. One hundred million American people now eat about a gallon and a half of this delicacy per capita yearly, and it takes the equivalent of 225,000,000 gallons of whole milk to make the annual supply.

During the past ten years the growth of ice cream manufacture has been remarkable, and the benefits it brings to the dairy industry, as shown recently by one big maker, seem to be unmistakable. For instance, he predicts that by the next census hardly any skimmilk will be sold; to-day we are selling less than one gallon where six gallons were sold in 1900. Ice cream has provided a comparatively new outlet for whole milk, so skimmilk need not be made in such quantities, and it is too valuable to sell or feed to stock in most localities.

The ice cream maker buys both cream and whole milk from the dairyman, and the cream generally brings better prices when made up into this more valuable product than when it is churned into butter. His demand has made milk prices more uniform the year round, it is said, because for five months in summer, when milk production is heaviest and keeping is most difficult, the ice cream business is booming. Quality also plays its part in the ice cream demand for dairy products, for higher standards are encouraged.

Ice cream stabilizes the market in another way. Condensed milk is an important ingredient in its manufacture, and 30,000,000 gallons of this product are used every year, or about one-quarter of our total product. Much of this condensed milk represents surplus, turned into that form when its sale as whole milk or cream would not be profitable. Hundreds of creameries have installed equipment for condensing surplus milk to sell to ice cream makers.

From the creamery standpoint ice cream gives a two-fold outlet. Many creameries make it themselves for sale to large customers, and where this is not feasible the ice cream industry, with a capital investment of somewhere between fifty and seventy-five million dollars, offers a stable market. So the cow and the ice cream freezer have much in common.

CONDENSED MILK

Condensed milk defined.— In 1856 a patent was granted to Gail Borden, Jr., on a process for " concentrating sweet milk by evaporation in vacuo, having no sugar or other foreign matter mixed with it." From small beginnings the business has grown to enormous proportions, and is still largely in the hands of the descendants of the original patentee. At the present time the condensed product is made both with or without sugar, and is sold in bulk or in hermetically sealed cans in which latter form it may be preserved for an indefinite time. By far the larger portion of the product is made with the addition of sugar, and is put up in cans.

The successful condensation of milk requires that the milk be produced under the best hygienic conditions and from the purest and most wholesome foods. Consequently we find among the patrons of condensing factories a highly developed state of dairy husbandry. Condensed milk is being used to a great extent in ice cream making with very satisfactory results. Some large factories have their own condensing machinery, by means of which they not only make their own filler, but convert any surplus milk into a product that may be stored until needed in their factory or disposed of through other channels. Plain evaporated milk in bulk is the grade of condensed milk commonly used for this purpose.

HOMOGENIZATION DEFINED

A homogenized cream is one which has been made homogeneous or identical throughout its entire mass by having been passed through a special apparatus which, under pressure of from 3,000 to 5,000 pounds per square inch, so breaks up the fat globules in the milk or cream as almost absolutely to prevent all cream from rising. It also makes it extremely difficult or impossible to do thorough skimming even by centrifugal force; neither may the cream be churned. But its viscosity is greatly increased, a change in character which obviously lends itself particularly well to do in ice cream making.

The homogenizing of cream is a new proposition in America; but it seems destined to have a future. Not the least interesting of the many things this new mechanism is capable of doing is the reuniting of an unsalted butter and skim milk to form a milk or a cream of any desired grade. This possibility offers enticing opportunities to those who are finding it increasingly difficult to provide the trade with sweet cream during certain portions of the year. Homogenized cream may be produced in three different ways, thus:

(1) By using natural cream.

(2) By mixing skim or whole milk and butter in such proportions that the resulting product will be cream of the desired per cent. of fat.

(3) By mixing butter, milk powder and water in such proportions that the resulting mixture will have approximately the same composition as the natural cream.

A good mixture for making homogenized cream is to use 16 pounds of dry skimmilk, 16 pounds butter and 68 pounds of water.

The homogenizing of milk and cream has been studied carefully and tests have been made giving the following results:

The Number of Bacteria was increased from 1,500,000 per c. c. to 11,500,030 per c. c. by homogenizing at temperatures sufficiently low as not to kill the bacteria present.

In commercial homogenization, however, the general practice of pasteurizing the milk at 185 degrees before homogenization destroys practically all bacteria present.

Homogenizing Cream Increases Its Viscosity. A 15 per cent. cream after being homogenized has the appearance of a 25 per cent. normal cream, and a 20 per cent. cream has the appearance of a 40 per cent. normal cream.

The Cooked Flavor imparted to milk and cream by pasteurizing at high temperatures is eliminated by homogenizing it.

The Keeping Quality of Milk or Cream pasteurized at 185 degrees was not affected in any way by homogenization. A number of samples of cream were kept for two weeks at a temperature near 50 degrees. The per cent. of acidity in the normal cream increased from .175 per cent. to .30 per cent., while that in the homogenized samples showed an increase of .165 per cent. to .26 per cent. Pasteurizing the cream at 185 degrees accounts for this slight increase in acidity. At the end of each week all the samples were unfit for consumption, due to off flavors.

Homogenized Cream Could Not Be Churned. Two lots of cream exactly alike, except that one had been homogenized, were churned in a small lightning churn at the same temperature. The normal cream churned readily in 12 minutes, the homogenized cream did not show the slightest change.

Repasteurizing Homogenized Cream destroyed the viscosity imparted by homogenization.

Ice Cream Made from Homogenized Cream possessed a much improved body, smoother texture and richer flavor.

Homogenized Cream when added to coffee did not mix so readily as normal cream, there being a slight evidence of feathering, making it appear sour. This objection was not found serious, however, until the acidity was above .20 per cent., though the normal cream did not feather with 25 per cent. acidity.

MILK POWDER

Milk powder has made quite a progress within the last few years. This product is used to replace fresh milk by many ice cream manufacturers. Three kinds of milk powders are manufactured: whole-milk powder, half-skimmed milk powder and skimmed milk powder. The butter fat in the whole-milk powder interferes with its keeping properties. The chief desirable advantages of reducing milk to a powder may be summed up as follows. This refers to milk powder made from skimmilk:

1. It is concentrated, making cost of package and transportation the minimum.

2. It has good keeping properties. Germs do not multiply in skim-milk powder, even at ordinary room temperature.

3. It is a dry substance, making it convenient to handle.

4. Milk powder is valuable to the ice cream manufacturer when there is a shortage of cream by the assistance of a homogenizer or an emulser.

HAUK'S EMULSER.

PASTEURIZATION

The thorough pasteurization of sweet cream destroys about 99 per cent. of bacteria present, and hence causes the cream to keep sweet a much longer time. But the heating of the cream breaks down the clusters of fat globules, renders the cream less viscous, and apparently poorer or lower in fat content. The ice cream maker desires a thick, viscous cream, so he generally objects to pasteurization. It has been found that when cream is allowed to stand at a low temperature (about 40 degrees Fahrenheit) for 24 hours after pasteurization it yields as large a volume of good bodied ice cream as does raw cream kept under similar temperature conditions for the same length of time. Hence pasteurized cream may be used successfully in ice cream making if it is allowed to reëstablish its viscosity.

SCHEMES FOR PAYING EXPENSES IN WINTER

One drawback in the wholesale ice cream business is the slow season, from the middle of September to the middle of the following May, and when the rush is over and the hot days have passed the manufacturer will say to himself, " What can I do to keep busy and pay expenses for the winter; I have horses, wagons, automobiles, plenty of time and a little money? "

We know of one firm that was in the ice cream business for eight years and in the fall of each year they laid off nearly all their help. One day the manager decided to go in the produce business in connection with the ice cream business; he said, " If we can sell our customers ice cream in the summer we can sell produce in the winter." This they done with success; they invested $500 for a carload of potatoes, they sold them all in a few days and then bought another carload and so on with other kinds of produce, and to-day this firm is receiving orders through the telephone for produce not only in winter but the summer also, and keeping all their rigs and help busy the whole year round. Potatoes should be bought by weight and sold by the barrel so as to realize a fair profit from them. It is the same as ice cream in one sense of the word, as you can buy sweet cream by the pound, beat it up into ice cream and sell it by the gallon. We suggest you hire some one to start you in this kind of a business who has had experience in that line before you venture, as it is a very interesting and tricky business.

We know of another ice cream firm who had fancy cards printed and hung up in hotels and cafes advertising their chocolate syrup to be used in milk chocolates for the bar trade. They worked up a fine business with 200 cafes using their chocolate syrups, and some of the places used about 5 gallons a day. It will cost about 40 cents a gallon to make and sell for $1 per gallon.

Another ice cream firm kept after the private house trade in the winter and worked up a fine trade by keeping an advertisement in the newspapers about their brick ice cream, stating that every week there would be a $5 gold piece placed in the center of one of the bricks, and people would continue ordering the cream to see if they were lucky enough to get a gold brick. The same firm had cards printed with a menu on them. The title of them were, "What to get for the Sunday dinner." On these cards there were suggestions for all kinds of fancy ice cream and ices, etc.

RETURNING EMPTY FREEZERS

Another important thing about the ice cream business is the cost of delivery and the loss of empties. Most of the large concerns figure that it costs approximately six cents to seven cents for each gallon of ice cream delivered; no doubt that these figures are correct when the wages of drivers and the cost of feed for the horses and the depreciation of cans and tubs, wagons and automobiles are taken in consideration.

One of the most difficult problems to solve for most ice cream dealers is, how can we avoid the loss of so many cans and tubs. Some will say charge them up to the drivers, others will say charge them to the customers, and others will advise you to go after them yourself.

We suggest that you allow so much of a discount every week to your store trade customers, providing they return them to the drivers washed and clean. No doubt a system of this kind could be worked out in some manner and it would not only save your cans from being lost, kept in cellars, and thrown on ash heaps in the back yards, but they would require less washing when they are returned to the factory.

In regard to the private trade when your rigs are all busy delivering ice cream and too busy to pick up empties, we suggest that you keep a good record of them, and at the end of each week or so, give a list of all your empties to some parcel delivery in your city and give him about five cents for every freezer he returns. If you have 100 empties scattered around the city no doubt he will be only too glad to earn $5, and with this system it would be cheaper than if you paid six cents each for paper pail carriers and gave them away with each order.

SCHEME FOR SAVING TIME WHILE TAGGING TUBS

Many progressive ice cream manufacturers are using this new invention in the form of a wire hook for the purpose of attaching tags on ice cream tubs. They give the freezers a neat appearance and save hours of time.

The old style system of strings and wires cost more money and are untidy. With this system of tagging freezers, shipments can be made from the factory, saving at least 15 seconds on each tub.

If 300 shipments are made a day and 15 seconds are saved on every tub, then one and one-quarter hours will be saved every day, which will be enough time and money saved during the season sufficient to buy all the tags and tag-hooks for the next season.

TESTING ICE CREAM FOR FAT

The testing of ice cream for butter fat in a manner applicable to the purposes of the factory is considerably more difficult than is the testing of ordinary milk or cream, because of the presence of the large amount of cane sugar. There are two or more methods for making such fat tests, which, though doubtless of value in chemical laboratories, are too complicated and tedious to be of the highest value in the factory where rapidity of work is a prime essential and where only approximately accurate results are required.

The following method has been used by the writer with
excellent results, the fat column being as clear and clean as
are those attained in ordinary work with milk or cream.
This method, or rather modification of an existing method,
although requiring care and close attention to details in
order to achieve satisfactory results, is not essentially
difficult.

Carefully weigh 18 grams of a well melted (but not over-
heated) and mixed sample of ice cream into a 30 per cent.
cream bottle. To this add four or five c. c. of lukewarm
water. Now add ordinary sulphuric acid, a little at a time,
thoroughly mixing the fluids with each addition. Little
more than half and seldom as much as two-thirds the usual
amount of acid is required; and not more than one-half of
this amount should be used at the outset, and some little
time should be allowed for it to act. If the color is not yet
that of strong coffee add a little more acid, shake and pause
for a time. If still the color is too light add yet more acid.
In this way the color is built up to the desired point. When
the contents of the bottle have assumed almost the desired
amber color add four or five c. c. of cool water to check the
further action of the acid. The test is thereafter conducted
as would be an ordinary cream test, care being taken that
the machine does not become too hot during whirling. If
this scheme is carefully followed, particularly in the matter
of the slow and gradual addition of the acid, the fat should
appear in the neck of the test bottle of a clear, light brown
color and distinct from the solution below. When this distinct, clean-cut condition has been obtained, the tester may
feel sure, provided the work has been in other respects

carried out in accord with the well-understood details of the Babcock method, that the results will be reasonably accurate.

STANDARDIZING MILK AND CREAM

When milks and creams of different tests are mixed together to determine a certain percentage of butter fat the following is a simple method by which calculations of this kind have been worked:

Draw a rectangle with two diagonals, as shown below. At the left hand corners place the tests of the milks or cream to be mixed. In the center place the richness desired. At the right hand corners place the differences between the two numbers in line with these corners. The number at the upper right hand corner represents the number of quarts of milk or cream to use with the richness indicated in the upper left hand corner. Likewise the number at the lower right hand corner represents the number of pounds of milk or cream to use, with the richness indicated in the lower left hand corner.

Example: How many quarts each of 30 per cent. cream and 3.5 per cent. milk required to make 25 per cent. cream?

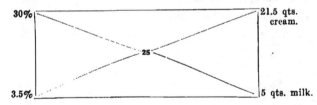

21.5, the difference between 3.5 and 25, is the number of quarts of 30 per cent. needed; and 5 the difference between

25 and 30 is the number of quarts of 3.5 per cent. milk needed.

From the ratio of milk and cream thus found any definite quantity is easily made up. If, for example, 300 quarts of 25 per cent. cream is desired, the number of quarts each of 30 per cent. cream and 3.5 per cent. milk is determined as follows:

$21.5+5=26.5.$

$$\frac{21.5}{26.5} \times 300 = 243.4,$$ the number of quarts of 30% cream.

$$\frac{5}{26.5} \times 300 = 56.6,$$ the number of quarts of 3.5% milk.

In calculating the percentage of butter-fat in a quantity of portions, for instance you have on hand the following quantities:

10 quarts of 20 per cent. cream.

5 quarts of　4 per cent. milk.

5 quarts of　6 per cent. condensed milk.

In order to find the percentage in all you may first multiply the quantity of cream by the amount of the given percentage and in the same manner with the milk and condensed milk, as follows:

10 times 20 equals 200

5 times　4 equals　20

5 times　6 equals　30

Total 250

After adding the amounts together then divide by total amount of quarts in mix. For instance:

$250 \div 20 = 12\frac{1}{2}.$

KEEPING CREAM SWEET

A can of cream or milk set into cold water will cool many times more rapidly than it will if set into a dry air refrigerator, even though the air and water were kept at the same temperature. This is due to the fact that water is a much better conductor of heat than is air and that the heat carrying capacity of the mass which is able to come into contact with the can is immensely greater in the case of water; in fact the amount of heat required to be absorbed from the article being cooled in order to raise the temperature of water one degree is 445 times greater than the amount of heat required to raise the temperature of the same volume of air one degree. Or, in other words, one cubic foot of water will absorb 445 times as much heat from the can of cream as will one cubic foot of air for each degree rise in temperature. And added to these facts is another equally important, namely, that it is next to impossible to cool the air of a refrigerator with ice much below 50 degrees, while the common temperature is about 55 degrees, which must be looked upon as merely the lower limit of normal souring, at which the growth of lactic acid bacteria will be slow but certain. On the other hand the temperature of water in which a few large chunks of ice are floating will be found to range from 34 degrees to 38 degrees. Thus cream set away to mature, yet to keep sweet, will not only cool much faster but also to a lower point if water is employed. This system, when a well-insulated tank is used, is not only the most efficient, for the reasons just given, but also the most economical of ice (that is, both the latent and the specific cold, if one may use the reversal term, which,

5

though perhaps coined, serves admirably the present need), will be employed for useful purposes instead of being largely wasted, as is the case when the cans of cream are merely packed close in a corner and buried with broken ice. When this is done, as is so often the case, the can is largely surrounded merely by cool air, and the ice cold water formed by the melting ice runs away to the sewer, still capable, however, of having done much good, quick work.

Housewives will do well to remember this principle when endeavoring to keep milk for children. Ordinarily clean market milk will keep sweet from two days to a week longer, or from two to three times longer if held in ice water than if held in the dry air of a kitchen ice chest or refrigerator. Another interesting point in this connection is that the entire ice box is cooled to a lower temperature when a part of the ice is put into a pail of water.

The greater cooling power of water over air, even of the same temperature, is nicely illustrated by the practice of blacksmiths, who systematically plunge hot iron into water to cool instead of waiting for it to cool in air. Many other familiar examples of this principle will be recalled by the reader.

FACTORS IN ICE CREAM MAKING

To our knowledge there has been but little published on research or other work done on ice cream. A Vermont bulletin covers considerable of the work done by the Vermont Experimental Station on Commercial Ice Cream. Monthly publications treat of many of the general questions confronting the manufacture of ice cream. Hammer, of the Iowa Experimental Station, gives a detailed report of bacteria in ice cream in his bulletin.

The work which we have taken up deals with the influence of gelatine, gum tragacanth and ice cream powders on the over-run in ice cream. Also the influence of brine temperatures on the over-run, the advantages and the disadvantages of three types of brine freezers — the vertical batch (Clad), horizontal batch, and the continuous machine. We also performed tests to determine the number of bacteria in the commercial ice cream. In our work we have also given a discussion of the present fat standards and attempted to show that these standards are unjustifiable.

The exact origin of ice cream is not definitely known. Some authorities credit the Italians as being the first to combine different ingredients, honey, fresh eggs and cream. This they froze in long, cylindrical shapes and served in wine glasses. Others credit the Germans as the first people to serve frozen dishes.

However, the Americans to-day lead in the manufacture of ice cream. In the past 15 years the growth of the ice cream industry has been marvelous. To-day the term ice cream covers a wide variety of frozen products. The ice creams of to-day may be highly flavored with vanilla, chocolate, berries and fruits. So-called binders, fillers and smootheners have attained a place of much importance in the ice cream industry. The food authorities of to-day, as well as the ice cream manufacturers, question very much the exact purpose and results of the use of the many fillers, binders and smootheners. Many fair arguments are presented for and against their use. Food authorities maintain that by the use of these different gelatinoid binders the manufacturer is able to conceal the age of his product. That the swell or increase in the volume of the frozen product is a result of their use. That a higher and often unsafe holding temperature is made possible.

On the other hand the manufacturer presents some very plausible arguments in favor of the use of these ingredients. First, it discourages the return of unsold goods, which would oftener be refrozen and sold again. Second, their use prevents the granulation or crystallation of watery portions of the cream. Third, it is maintained that gelatine and vegetable gum do not increase the swell in ice cream.

Faults in the Fat Standards of Ice Cream. Ice cream is sold by the dish, pint, quart or gallon. It is never sold by weight, yet the statutes of many states provide for a percentage test by weight, or that on the basis of the Babcock test, ice cream shall contain a given per cent. of fat.

The amount of fat in a measured quantity of ice cream may vary and still the per cent. of fat be the same. If, for example, two different gallons of ice cream were taken, the per cent. of fat in each may be the same and still the amount of fat in separate gallons would or could be widely different. When the ingredients of ice cream are ready to be frozen the manufacturer refers to it as his mix or mixture, and all the mixtures are referred to or figured on the basis of a 10-gallon batch, or 10 gallons of finished product. To make 10 gallons of ice cream some manufacturers use 5 gallons of a mix, some use six, seven and some eight and some nine, and in the freezing process the mix, no matter what amount was to start with, he tries to whip that amount up to make 10 gallons of frozen cream. This is often resorted to by the manufacturer who make different grades of cream.

Assuming that the various mixtures have the same weight per gallon, say 10 pounds, then take 5 gallons or 50 pounds of 12 per cent. mix to make 40 quarts of finished product, and the finished product will weigh 5 pounds to the gallon and each gallon will contain six-tenths of a pound of butter fat. Or take any of the following:

"A." Six gallons of 12 per cent. mix; this will weigh 60 pounds, each gallon will contain .72 pounds of fat, or 40 quarts will contain 72 pounds of fat.

" B." If 7 gallons of mix be used at 12 per cent. fat the mix will contain 84 pounds of fat; if this be whipped to 40 quarts each gallon will contain .84 pounds of fat.

" C." If 8 gallons be taken as a mix at 12 per cent. the mix will contain 96 pounds of fat, and this whipped to 40 quarts, will allow each gallon to contain .96 pounds of fat per gallon.

The above shows conclusively that a statement or declaration of the per cent. butter fat does not inform as to the amount of fat that the buyer receives in his plate, pint, quart or gallon. It seems in this respect that the fat standard as now used in ice cream is useless to the public.

Not only ice creams with the same percentage of fat vary as to the amount in a measured quantity, but ice creams with the same amount of fat in measured quantities may vary in the per cent. of fat.

Take a 5-gallon mix weighing 50 pounds with a fat content of 12 per cent. and make into 40 quarts of finished product; the finished product will weigh 5 pounds to the gallon and each gallon will contain .6 pounds per gallon.

Then take 6 gallons of 11 per cent. mix; this will contain .66 pounds of fat; make this into 40 quarts and each gallon will contain .66 pounds of fat, practically the same amount as in the first case.

If a 5-gallon mix is taken to make 40 quarts of ice cream, which will pass as legal, and to this mix 4 gallons of whole milk are added, 40 quarts of finished product are produced, we increase the amount of butter fat in each gallon, but the per cent. of fat is so reduced as to make the product illegal.

From the above discussion we have attempted to prove that the fat standards are not justifiable if the per cent. of cream is to be figured on the basis of the weight of ice cream.

In conducting the freezing in our experiments every care was taken to have conditions correspond, unless a varying factor was necessary to demonstrate the problem of the experiment.

The formula used in making a mix was:

   40 pounds of 25 per cent. cream.
   20 pounds of 4 per cent. milk.
   10 pounds of sugar.
   3½ ounces of flavor extract.
   One or more of the fillers, or no filler at all.

With the above mix it was possible to get two freezings with an approximate weight of 71 pounds each, thus eliminating any experimental error due to difference in the volume of the batch.

The temperature of the ice cream was used as the point of drawing the frozen product. This temperature was about 26 degrees to 28 degrees F.

TABLE SHOWING EFFECT OF BRINE TEMPERATURE ON THE
OVERRUN, BODY AND TEXTURE OF ICE CREAM.

Type of machine used	Brine temperature	Time to freeze	Overrun	Body and texture
	Deg. F.	Min.	Per cent.	
Vertical batch............	13–14	18	50	Icy, firm.
(Clad).................	18–20	20	55	Icy, buttery, firm
(Clad).................	12–14	17	50	Icy, (no filler used).
	18–20	21	56	Icy, (no filler used).
	14–16	19	52	Smooth, firm.
Aged 24 hours..........	18–22	23	60	Smooth, buttery, firm.
	14–16	19	53	Smooth, firm.
	10–12	15	48	Very icy, no filler.
	10–12	16	48	Very icy, no filler.
	10–12	15	47	Smooth, firm.
	18–20	21	55	Smooth, firm, buttery.
	18–20	20	55	Smooth, firm, buttery.
Aged 24 hours..........	10–12	14	53	Smooth, firm.
	10–12	15	53	Smooth, firm.
	8–10	12	54	Very smooth, firm.
Aged 24 hours...........	20–22	22	56	Buttery, firm.
	10–12	14	45	Firm, smooth.
Aged 24 hours..........	23	25	68	Loose..

In the few runs made with a horizontal batch machine, the point that the per cent. overrun is to a great extent dependent on the brine temperature is illustrated. With 10 degrees as a low temperature a swell of 50 per cent. was obtained; on raising to a brine temperature of 20 degrees a swell of 70 per cent. was obtained at the expense of the body and texture.

INFLUENCE OF BRINE TEMPERATURE ON OVERRUN, BODY AND
TEXTURE OF ICE CREAM.

Type of machine	Temperature of brine	Time to freeze brine	Overrun	Body and texture
	Deg. F.	Min.	Per cent.	
Horizontal batch.........	10–11	15	55	Very good.
	18–20	21	74	Loose, flaky.
	10–12	16	57	Good, firm, smooth.
Continuous..............	15	22	60	Fair.
	20	18	70	Loose, flaky.

The tabulated data on the influence of brine temperature on overrun, body and texture when the batch machine was used, proves conclusively that the overrun obtained is dependent very much on the brine temperature, a low temperature causing a low overrun and a higher temperature a higher overrun. In all the experiments this point was brought out quite conclusively. The minimum overrun obtained with this machine was 45 per cent., with a brine temperature of 10–12 degrees F., while the maximum overrun was 68 per cent., with a brine temperature of 23 degrees F.

The difference in the brine temperature in the two freezings was about 10 degrees, while the difference in the per cent. overrun was 24.

The per cent. overrun obtained in none of the freezings with the vertical batch was so great as to cause a loose and undesirable texture; the general freezing with this machine was a firm, smooth product, unless no filler was used, when a tendency toward iciness was shown. In the runs with a higher temperature (19–23) butter lumps were also present, due to the prolonged freezing period. This undesirable feature could be eliminated by lowering the initial temperature of the mix to at least 38 degrees F.

In using the disc machine the influence on brine temperature on overrun, body and texture is more apparent.

In this machine the peculiar beating of the cream is conducive to a high overrun. The per cent. of the mix exposed to the freezing surface is much greater than in other types of machines, allowing a longer freezing period, and also eliminating the danger of butter lumps in the finished product.

In all experiments with this machine the point was brought out that a high brine temperature is inducive to

a high per cent. overrun. With a minimum brine temperature of 10 degrees, and a low overrun of 55 per cent., the
per cent. overrun was increased with each raise in the
brine temperature, until at a temperature of 22 degrees an
overrun of 78 per cent. was obtained. The influence of brine
temperature on the body and texture of ice cream was
brought out strongly here. When an overrun of more than
68 per cent. was obtained the finished product was loose
and flaky, and could not be classed as a salable ice cream.
After standing in storage tanks much of the excessive swell
was lost, and in any case of repacking the loss in volume
would be enormous.

SANITARY ICE CREAM FACTORIES

For years the national and state ice cream associations
have carried on their programs and talks for the production of clean ice cream factories, and they have proven all
the advantages of sanitation. Reams of stuff have been
printed on the same subject and one would think that every
reading ice cream manufacturer would be impressed with
the importance of the subject. Unfortunately there are
many manufacturers who have paid little attention to the
value of clean and wholesome ice cream.

Several states have passed sanitary codes and if the authorities will get busy they can make the slipshod men clean
up. It is up to the authorities in those states. If a state
has no specific ice cream code it doesn't follow that there
should be ice cream below standard. General health laws
everywhere are strong enough to compel the shiftless ones
to change their methods.

There are in all the large cities many aliens who have gone into the ice cream industry. As a class these men know nothing about sanitation and are careless. They ought to be cleaned out unless they will conform to the American idea of sanitation. They can be stopped by the authorities. The foreigners do not in general read the trade papers, nor do they join trade associations, so they have very little chance to learn the modern methods that have placed ice cream in general on such a high plane.

It is hard to say that the foreigners are not the only ones on which the heavy hand of law ought to fall. There are several big concerns in the country that are too stingy to put their plants on a sanitary basis. These people know better and some of them are represented in the councils of the national association. Their plants ought to be shut up first of all. When a concern is making a pot of money each year and still runs plants that it dares not open to the public it is high time it were put out of business. There is no excuse for such concerns.

Ice cream has become such a universal article of consumption in this country that it has attracted attention from the public. So much is invested in the business that one knock by the authorities can injure the investment of an individual concern. For those who have invested small fortunes in modern, sanitary factories there is only one course to pursue in this matter. To protect themselves the conscientious manufacturers ought to investigate the plants of competitors and point out changes that should be made to insure a clean wholesome ice cream. Do it in fairness. Don't be captious, but firmly tell the delinquent that unless he follows the code on the best methods in vogue in sanitary plants that you will complain to the board of health.

In this way you will protect your own investment and the good name of ice cream in general. A good many think this is a harsh method, but I believe it is better than going to the board of health with your suspicions. Your complaints will be misconstrued and maybe nothing will be done. If anything is done it will get into the papers and ice cream will get a black eye in your city.

Nine times out of ten the advice and admonition of a recognized leader in the trade will be taken by the delinquent. You then have made a friend instead of an enemy of a competitor and have saved ice cream from hurtful publicity. In case you cannot succeed in making the dirty man clean up you can then go to the board of health with a story that will be listened to with thanks. Is this not the fairest way to handle the situation?

There are many ice cream men that do not learn anything until they are shown just what to do. Laws and codes do not teach them. They never go to conventions and pay little heed to what they read — if they read at all. These men would clean up if some one would tell them how to do it. Who is better qualified to impart this information than the ice cream man who has worked out the problem? Certainly the inspector cannot do as well as the manufacturer, for the former does not understand the practical end of the business.

In several states the ice cream sanitary code was written by the manufacturers themselves and adopted by the authorities without a change. That proves the good intent of the leaders who made ice cream a household word. It also shows that the authorities realize that the industry is on a high plane. It is a fact that the men who have worked out a sanitary plan in their factories demand more of their competitors than the authorities would suggest.

There have been complaints from the unthinking and backward manufacturers that the sanitary codes put over are for the purpose of putting them out of business. It is not so at all. The leaders realize that the public demands clean ice cream and if the manufacturers do not provide it every one is liable to be hit. They have moved in the matter first to protect the name of the product and secondly to protect their own investment. If the manufacturers did not aid the authorities in proposing a practical plan of sanitation the authorities would propose an impractical plan. Something is bound to be put in force by the leaders, having the practical experience.

The Sanitary Code of New York, for instance, is not half as hard to follow as it would appear. This code is serving as a model for other states and it ought to be adopted in every state. There is nothing visionary in it and nothing but common sense. It does not impose hardships on any manufacturer. In fact, it shows the manufacturer the easiest, quickest and cheapest way to meet modern conditions. As such it is a model, not only for the ice cream trade, but other food lines.

Sunlight and ventilation are the first requisites for a sanitary factory. The best germicide known to science is the rays of the sun, and they are especially efficacious where milk is used. The sun will dissipate milk odor better than any amount of cleaning powder. Of course proper ventilation goes hand in hand with the influx of sunlight in keeping a plant sweet and free from odors.

There are few food products that have the advantage of such perfect equipment as ice cream. The modern freezer and mixer, with the take down piping, are almost perfect in a sanitary way. After being installed it is up to the owner to keep the equipment clean and sweet. Plenty of pure cold water and hot water are necessities in an ice cream plant, and the use of steam is a desirable adjunct. If the mixer, piping and freezer are thoroughly flushed after every day's run, first with cold water, then hot water or steam; and, if the mixer and freezer are scrubbed with a washing compound three times a week and the piping taken down and scrubbed out at least twice a week the product will be wholesome and clean.

The mixing room and freezer room should be inclosed and have walls and floors that will admit of being flushed with ease. Of course large drains are essential. This keeps dust down and if flies are kept out of these rooms there will be little danger of contamination as far as methods go. A flyless and dustless plant is a thing to be strived for. It is not difficult to attain.

The greatest care should be exercised to keep all the cans clean. A lick and a promise is the policy of the careless manufacturer, while the careful man insists upon absolutely clean cans, perfectly dried and dustless before they are filled. There are can washers on the market that answer the purpose, but the small manufacturer need not buy them, for he can with a tank and brush keep them clean. The tank should have cold and hot water connections, and a cleansing compound should be used. A couple

of rinsings in hot water will finish the job. Elbow grease
is necessary when the hand method is used.

It must be remembered that no matter how sanitary your
equipment is you will fail unless your method is right.
Insist upon cleanliness throughout the plant. Compel the
workmen to be clean or get men who will be. Keep at them
all the time on this subject; make it the first law for holding the job. A clean white suit donned every day is part
of the campaign to instill your ideas in the minds of the
workmen. Have closets for keeping brooms, mops and the
like — don't have them left around in sight. Have racks
for the hose and allow nothing under foot.

The prohibition of tobacco in the plant and that of touch-
ing the cream or product by the hands are two essential
features that seem to be appreciated least by the manufacturer. Tobacco smoke will taint cream quicker than anything else. There is no sense in dipping your finger into a
can of cream to see if it is sweet. Have a glass of water
and a spoon handy. Especial care should be used in making bricks and fancy moulds. Workmen should wash their
hands in hot water every few minutes and dry them on
clean towels. The ordinary workman will rub off the grease
on his overalls if he isn't watched. That is a dirty practice.

Common sense should be used by the owner and he should
make a fad of cleanliness. His workmen soon will become
so impregnated with the idea that they will fear to have anything that the owner will criticise. While there is no chance
for contamination to the ice cream on the wagon if the contents of the cans are covered with parchment paper under
the cover, it pays to have the wagons and tubs spick and
span. With the driver clad in white and with a team that is

bright and clean looking, the attention of persons on the street is attracted. This is an advertisement that should not be overlooked.

One of the largest manufacturers in Chicago always had a fad for fine teams. He has won several medals in the work horse day parade. This was an advertisement that paid. His competitors took up the idea and now a slovenly team is rare in Chicago. If you run autos see that they are clean and bright. A large concern in New York pays little attention to its teams and cars. The horses evidently are picked for cheapness and are seldom groomed as they should be. The wagons are painted in the winter and from lack of care they look horrible by July. The autos are neg- lected and are anything but a favorable advertisement. It can be said that these teams and cars reflect the condi- tion of the plants where the food product is made.

The enterprising manufacturer is the clean manufac- turer, and the rule works both ways. Cleanliness costs little after the plant is equipped; in fact, it costs less than to neglect the machinery in the long run.

Each manufacturer must learn a lesson. He can show the way to sanitation if he chooses, or he can wait until some inspector comes along and condemns his plant. The ad- verse publicity will be a bitter pill to swallow, but it will serve the slothful and careless manufacturer right.

BRICK ICE CREAM

In making stock bricks use the large 6-quart slab brick moulds which are cut up after being turned out of the mould, and can be filled direct from freezer or 10-gallon cans after the freezing is done. To make a perfectly straight lined three layer or metropolitan brick put a layer of either strawberry or chocolate, filling the mould one-third full and level off and set perfectly level in air blast room to harden. If the ice cream is not hard what is in the mould should be hard enough to bear the next layer in from twenty to thirty minutes, which should be put on as carefully and evenly as possible and in not too large quantities at a time or it may break through the crust on the under layer and make uneven places in the layers. The second layer should be leveled with trowel and again put to harden, after which the mould against should be filled with another flavor of ice cream full enough to press out under the edges of lid when it is put on as this seals the mould and prevents the water from entering when it is dipped in the water to soften the edges of the ice cream so the slab will fall out; this makes a beautiful three-layered brick. The moulds should have a three-eighths hole punched in the center of the bottom over which you place a small piece of wax paper when filling; this admits the air when turning out the brick slab and lets it slide out easily, otherwise it cannot get air and comes out with difficulty.

The bricks can be partly filled one day and finished the next if more convenient, or the filling can be extended over three days, one layer a day if necessary. After the bricks are cut they should be wrapped in wax or parchment paper and placed in pasteboard brick boxes to make a neat package. There are several styles of brick ice cream boxes on the market.

In making up small special orders for brick ice cream, the most practical way in making them is to use the one-quart size brick moulds, that is, the ones with the double lids, as

SUGGESTIVE ADVERTISEMENT
FOR BRICK ICE CREAM

SANITARY ICE CREAM IN A SANITARY PACKAGE FROM A SANITARY FACTORY ARE NOT THE ONLY REASONS TO ACCOUNT FOR THE LARGE VOLUME OF ICE CREAM WE SELL IN THE COLD WINTER TIME. :: :: ::

Order one of our delicious, refreshing and wholesome bricks of pure ice cream. We deliver them in neat, small refrigerator pails. There will be no mussing in salt or ice like the old fashioned way of receiving ice cream. We have a better cream, better service and a better package.

UP-TO-DATE ICE CREAM CO.
BOSTON, MASS.

they are preferable to the ones with single lids, being easier to remove the cream. Special small orders of this type are moulded in practically the same manner as the large ones previously mentioned.

FANCY INDIVIDUAL ICE CREAM FORMS

Fancy ice cream forms, such as flowers, fruit, animals, toys, etc., are made by placing the various colors of ice cream into moulds which are made special for this purpose. They can be obtained from most all supply houses.

In order to make a perfect design it requires a certain amount of good judgment of the maker in selecting the proper colored creams to correspond with the design which is to be made.

The first operation is to fill the moulds with ice cream sufficiently to leave a certain amount remaining around the edges of the lid, as to prevent any salt water from entering. Pack them in salt and ice for about one hour, or sufficient time to harden.

To remove the ice cream simply dip them in lukewarn water and open and remove the ice cream very carefully with the aid of something sharp, some use a fork for this purpose.

After they have been removed in this manner they are to be wrapped in wax paper and then placed into square brick ice cream cans and packed for shipment.

Such designs as flowers and fruit are generally decorated with green leaves which will greatly add to the appearance of them. All fancy forms should be served by placing them on paper doilies.

A FEW HELPFUL SUGGESTIONS

Most large ice cream manufacturers declare that it cost less to make shipments out of town than it does to deliver around the city, especially when packing wagons are being used. It seems to be more convenient to have the express company bring the ice cream to the railroad station and return with the empties.

The proper way to figure the cost of delivery per gallon is as follows: If 75,000 gallons of ice cream are sold and delivered in one year, and the cost of delivery is $4,500, that is to say, the wages for drivers, feed for horses, repairs on wagons, and depreciation, the cost of delivery should be divided by the number of gallons and the result will be the cost per one gallon. Example, $4,500 ÷ 75,000 gal.= 6¢ per gal.

When packing cans of ice cream in salt and ice for storage in factories where there is no hardening room it is advisable to use thin square sheets of wax paper of different colors and placed over the cream before putting on the covers so the edges of the paper will extend out a little. For instance, use red paper for strawberry ice cream, white for vanilla, brown for chocolate, and this will enable you to distinguish one kind of ice cream from another without taking off the covers while they are buried in the ice. Wax paper should always be placed over the ice cream as it looks better to the customers, it is more sanitary, it keeps the rusty covers from soiling the cream, it also keeps the salt out of the cream when the covers are taken off suddenly.

When wrapping up brick ice cream for cardboard boxes it is always handy to have the correct dimensions wax paper on hand. The different size paper used by most dealers for standard quart bricks and pints or when the quarts are cut in halves and used for pints are: For quarts, 10½ x 14 inches, and pints, 6 x 8¾ inches.

When the cans are rusty and need scouring it is advisable to use wire wool; the same can be bought in any paint store.

The brine box of the ice-cream freezer, if a brine machine is being used, should be cleaned out at least once a month by removing the dirt from the bottom that settles there from the ice and salt; it is also advisable to pump hot water and lye or potash through the pipes which will clean them out thoroughly and avoid a crust from forming in the cells of the freezer. If this is done better results can be obtained.

MECHANICAL REFRIGERATION SIMPLIFIED

The introduction of mechanical refrigeration into the ice cream industry marked a new era in this line of business, and, as a matter of fact, brought a revolution in the arrangement of buildings and equipment in a very sanitary way. There is really no limit to the advantages which can be obtained from a plant with a modern cold storage room, etc., over the old style method of using salt and ice. Mechanical refrigeration for the ice cream dealer proves efficiency and is positively more economical than the old method. It has developed to such an extent in the large cities that it is a hard matter to compete with firms with modern equipped plants without a dry storage room.

Among the first questions asked by persons who are becoming interested in the subject of mechanical refrigeration or ice making, is " Tell me, if you will, how do you produce such an intense degree of cold by machinery? "

Permit us to briefly review the principal features, and aim to do it in a way that those who claim no particular knowledge of physics and thermodynamics may readily follow.

Mechanical refrigeration. This is produced primarily by the evaporation of a volatile liquid which will vaporize at low temperatures. By means of special apparatus the intensity and desired amount of refrigeration are entirely under the control of the operator.

The simplest form of apparatus consists of three principal parts:

A. An " evaporator," or as it is sometimes called, a " congealer," in which the volatile liquid is vaporized.

B. Combined suction and pressure pump, which sucks, or more properly speaking, " aspirates," from the evaporator, as fast as it is formed, the gas which is created thereby.

C. A liquefier, or, as it is commonly called, " condenser," into which this gas is discharged by the compressor pump, and under the combined action of the pump pressure and cold condenser, the vapor is here reconverted into a liquid to be taken up and used again in the evaporator or congealer.

Refined anhydrous liquid ammonia, from which every impurity has been eliminated, is the cold-producing agent which is generally used. "Anhydrous " means free from water, but there are a few other things to be rejected before a pure liquid may be obtained.

The office of the compressor pump and condenser is to reconvert the gas into a liquid after evaporation, thus mak-

SMOOTH RUNNING DEKALB COMPRESSOR.

ing the original charge of ammonia available for use in the same apparatus over and over again.

It may appear to the reader, after having carefully followed the text, that the pump and condenser might be dispensed with, but such a condition may be only economically realized when expensive liquid ammonia can be obtained in great quantities, and therefore at less cost than the process of reconverting the vapor on the spot into a liquid by compression machinery.

The real index to the amount of cooling work possible is the number of pounds of evaporated between the observed range of temperature.

To make this statement clear, each pound of ammonia during evaporation is capable of taking from the surrounding atmosphere, and storing up, a certain quantity of heat, so that really in its simplest form, a refrigerating apparatus might consist of but two parts — a tank of ammonia and an evaporator or congealer. With this apparatus the ammonia would be allowed to escape from the tank into the evaporator or congealer as fast as the coils therein were capable of evaporating the liquid into a gas when completely expanded; the resulting vapor would be allowed to escape into the atmosphere, which would mean total waste, and the supply would have to be maintained through fresh tanks of ammonia — a simple process, and yet tremendously expensive, and which would aggregate an expense of about $200 per ton refrigerating capacity.

It will be seen that to recover this gas, reconvert it into a liquid on the spot, and in a comparatively inexpensive manner, thereby using it over and over again, instead of using fresh ammonia, is the function of the compressor pumps and condensers.

The successful action of all refrigerating machinery depends upon well-defined natural laws which govern in all cases, no matter what type of apparatus or machine is used, the principle being the same in all, though the process may vary slightly. Of course, the properties of the particular agent and manner of its use affect the efficiency or economic results obtainable.

Most companies use anhydrous ammonia exclusively, let us confine ourselves strictly to this agent, stating meanwhile that it is only one of many substances that may be used, but so far none other which has been experimented with has proved so well adapted to the purpose.

A vessel of liquid ammonia thrust into a snow bank at a temperature of 32 degrees (which is 60½ degrees above its boiling point) would bear about the same relation to the snow bank as a vessel of water of ordinary temperature thrown into a fire. In both these cases there would result an evaporation of the liquid and absorption of heat by the resulting vapor.

It will perhaps make this plainer when we state that the heat required to evaporate the ammonia is taken from the snow bank, and the latter is thus made even colder through the absence of this heat than it was before.

Ammonia is composed of one part of nitrogen and three parts hydrogen. It can be obtained from the air, from sal-ammoniac, nitrogenous constituents of plants and animals by process of distillation — as a matter of fact, there are very few substances free from it.

At the present day almost all the sal-ammoniac and ammonia liquors are prepared from ammoniacal liquid, a by-product obtained in the manufacture of coal gas.

PROPERTIES OF AMMONIA

Pure ammonia liquid is colorless, having a peculiar alkaline odor and caustic taste. It turns red litmus paper blue. Its boiling point depends on its purity, and is about $28\frac{4}{10}$ degrees below zero at atmospheric pressure. Compared with water, its weight or specific gravity at 32 degrees Fahrenheit is about $\frac{5}{8}$ of water, or 0.6364. One cubic foot of liquid ammonia weighs 39.73 pounds, one gallon weighs $5\frac{1}{10}$ pounds and one pound of the liquid at 32 degrees will occupy 21.017 cubic feet of space when evaporated at atmospheric pressure. The specific heat of ammonia gas, as determined by Regnault (capacity for heat), is 0.50836. Its latent heat of evaporation, as determined by the highest authorities, is not far from 560 thermal units at 32 degrees, at which temperature one pound of liquid, evaporated under a pressure of 15 pounds per square inch, will occupy 21 cubic feet.

DIRECTIONS FOR INSTALLING, CHARGING AND OPERATING INCLOSED TYPE OF AMMONIA COMPRESSION MACHINES

INSTALLING

The compressor, condenser and receiver should be located in a dry and well-lighted place where they will be accessible at all times for inspection and repairs. The liquid receiver and connections should not be placed in the engine or boiler room, as the heat will evaporate part of the liquid and drive gas back into the condenser to be recondensed. Such an arrangement makes it necessary to install a larger condenser and to use more condensing water, and, in addition, the liquid goes into the evaporating system carrying its full quota of heat, thereby reducing its value.

The machine should be set on a well-built brick or concrete foundation, care being taken to have the machine perfectly level.

Before making the pipe connections all dirt and scale should be removed from the inside of the pipe and a pipe die run lightly over all threads exposed during shipment, after which they should be thoroughly washed with gasoline or benzine. The pipe fittings should be cleaned in the same way before connections are made. After the pipe and fittings have been thoroughly cleaned, apply a paste of litharge and glycerine to the threads and screw the pipe fittings up tight. Where soldered joints are required the threads on the pipe ends and fittings should be heated and thinned with solder before they are made up.

When the machine is in place and all pipe connections properly made, remove the cover of the crank case and fill with ammonia oil to the level of the crank shaft, or to the line on the frame of the compressor indicating the proper amount of oil required.

Disconnect the by-pass piping and close the main suction and discharge valves. Run the machine under no-load conditions for two hours to smooth up the bearings and make any adjustments that may be found necessary; then connect the by-pass on the discharge side. (Some manufacturers provide plugs in the by-pass piping, in which case it is not necessary to disconnect the piping.) Open the main discharge valve and all other valves on the ammonia system except the main suction valve and the by-pass valves, which should be closed.

Now start the machine again and pump air on the entire system to a pressure of about 150 pounds on the low-pressure gage. This should not be done, however, in one operation, on account of the possibility of melting the joints, due to the heat contained in the air. During the operation the machine should be stopped from time to time and all the apparatus examined in order to see that no undue heating occurs. Should parts of the apparatus be found unduly hot, the machine should remain at rest until the heated part is sufficiently cooled. Stop the machine and examine all piping and connections for leaks. This can best be done by applying soapsuds with a brush to all connections, and if there are any leaks they will be indicated by bubbles. If there is an ice-freezing tank in connection with the system, run water into the tank, completely submerging the coils, and if there are any leaks they may be detected by air bubbles rising from the joints.

If the ammonia system has been found to be tight at the pressure of 150 pounds, close all expansion valves and again start the machine and pump air to a gage pressure of about 275 pounds, unless the discharge pipe gets very hot. As the low-pressure gage will not register so high a pressure as 275 pounds, it should be cut off when it has reached the limit of its scale. Allow the system to remain under this pressure for several hours and if the loss in pressure as shown by the gage, does not exceed five pounds, the system may be considered satisfactory so far as leakage is concerned.

Remove the short pieces of pipe between the suction valve and the machine and allow the air under pressure to escape quickly through the suction valve. Any dirt and scale that may be in the piping and which would otherwise be drawn into the machine with the suction gas will be blown out.

Before the system is charged with the refrigerant it is necessary to remove all air and moisture; otherwise the efficient operation of the machine will be seriously interfered with. Manufacturers usually provide special valves for discharging the air from the system, which is accomplished by starting up the machine and pumping the air out, the operation being just the reverse of that when working under service conditions. When a vacuum of about 26 inches has been obtained, stop the machine again and allow it to stand for several hours in order to determine if the system will maintain a vacuum. If the vacuum is maintained, the system is ready to be charged with the ammonia.

It is impossible in some cases to remove all the air from the system by means of the compressor, in which case it is desirable to insert the proper amount of refrigerant gradually. Often from 60 to 70 per cent. of the full charge is inserted, and the air remaining in the system is allowed to escape through the purgecocks on the condenser until the ammonia shows, which will be detected by the very strong odor, and the escaping vapor will have the appearance of steam. An additional quantity of ammonia should then be inserted. This should be repeated once or twice a day until all the air has been displaced and the complete charge has been introduced.

CHARGING

To charge the machine, a drum of anhydrous ammonia is connected by a suitable pipe to the charging valve on the liquid receiver. Allow ammonia to enter the system through

VERTICAL INCLOSED SINGLE ACTING MACHINE, BELT DRIVEN, BUILT BY THE
YORK MANUFACTURING CO.

the charging valve until a pressure of about 15 pounds is recorded on the gage and then turn on the condensing water and start up the machine slowly at first. The suction and discharge valves should be wide open while the machine is being charged. When one tank is emptied the charging valve should be closed and another tank placed in position, this being repeated until the system is sufficiently charged for work, when the charging valve should be closed and the main expansion valve adjusted. The ammonia drums should be weighed before and after being emptied or partially emptied, and a record kept of the amount necessary for charging. The glass gage on the liquid receiver will show the amount of liquid contained, and the pressure gages, as well as the gradual cooling of the brine in the refrigerator and the frost collecting on the expansion pipe, will indicate when a sufficient amount of the refrigerant has been inserted to start working.

OPERATING

After the machine has been started and the expansion valve adjusted, the temperature of the delivery pipe should be carefully noted, and should a tendency to heat be observed, the expansion valve should be opened wider, while, on the other hand, if it should become cold, the valve should be slightly closed, the adjustment being continued until the temperature of the pipe is the same as that of the cooling water leaving the condenser. If there is an insufficient charge of the refrigerant, the delivery pipe will become heated, even though the expansion valve is wide open.

Some of the signs which indicate the proper working of the plant, other than the fact that it is satisfactorily performing its refrigerating functions, are: The vibrations of the pointers on the high and low pressure gages; the frost on the exterior surface of the refrigerating pipes; the liquid refrigerant can be plainly heard passing through the expansion valve; and the difference in temperature between the liquid leaving the condenser and the final temperature of the cooling water, and between the refrigerator and the brine.

Should it become necessary to disconnect any part of the ammonia system for any reason, the ammonia must be pumped out of that part and stored in another part of the system. After making repairs, all the air must be exhausted from that part of the system before the ammonia is again allowed to enter.

To pump ammonia out of the condenser. Close valves in the liquid pipe, the main suction, and discharge valves, and open the by-pass valves after draining the water from the condenser to prevent freezing and bursting of the pipes. Start the machine and pump out the ammonia until a partial vacuum is indicated by the high-pressure gage; then stop the machine and allow it to stand for two or three hours in order that any liquid ammonia lying in the pipes may have time to evaporate. Start up the machine again and pump down to a 25-inch vacuum. After all ammonia has been exhausted from the system, close the valve in the ammonia discharge pipe and the condenser may then be disassembled.

To pump the air out of condenser. The main suction and discharge valves should remain closed. The by-pass valve on the discharge side must be open and the one on the suction side closed. Manufacturers provide some means of opening the by-pass piping, either by a pipe tee or some form of cock; this should be opened and the machine run until all air is exhausted from the condenser. After all air has been exhausted the opening in the discharge by-pass must be closed and all valves set as they were originally. Ammonia may now be allowed to re-enter the condenser, and after turning on the cooling water the plant is again ready for operation.

To pump ammonia out of cold storage room or cooler coils. All expansion valves must be closed, also the suction stop valves, except the suction stop valve on the coil which it is desired to pump out. This valve must be left open and the machine run until a 10 or 15-inch vacuum is obtained, when the machine should be stopped for two hours in order to allow any remaining liquid in the coils to evaporate. After the evaporation of the remaining liquid, start the machine again and pump down to a 25-inch vacuum. If all liquid has evaporated and the ammonia valves are tight, the coils should maintain the 25-inch vacuum until broken. The suction and discharge valves on the machine may now be closed and the part of the system which has been pumped out may be opened with safety.

To pump air out of storage rooms or cooling coils. See that the main discharge stop valve is closed and remove the plug from tee or open cock, as the case may be, in the by-pass just below the discharge stop valve. The machine should be started slowly and run until all the air is exhausted from the coils, then stop machine and replace plug in tee or close cock in the by-pass.

To pump out compressor. The same method as above is followed, except that the suction stop valve only is closed, as no part of the system except the compressor is to be pumped out.

CONSTRUCTION AND LOCATION OF COLD STORAGE ROOMS

In the construction of cold storage rooms consideration should be given to the relations that the lateral dimensions bear to the cubical space of the room. This is an important factor in the construction of refrigerators and is one to which but little attention is given. It is important that the shape of the room should be given first consideration, and unless there are some local conditions that compel a different arrangement it should be built, as nearly as possible, in the form of a cube. This will present the smallest exterior surface for a given cubical space for any practical form of construction. For very small rooms, however, of less than 1,000 cubic feet capacity, it is impracticable to build them in the form of a cube, as the height should be 10 or 12 feet. This height affords a better circulation of air, and consequently a more uniform temperature, a purer, drier air, and more satisfactory refrigeration.

Where mechanical refrigeration is employed this height is necessary in order to provide space for the coil bunkers unless wall coils are used, in which case the height may be less. The circulation of air, however, is not so good with wall coils as with a bunker loft. If very cold temperatures are not required, as in the case of ordinary ice boxes, a lower room may answer the purpose. As an illustration of the saving of material in construction and in refrigeration, let us consider two cold storage rooms, each of 1,000 cubic feet capacity; one room to be in the form of a perfect cube, 10 by 10 by 10 feet = 1,000 cubic feet; the other room to be 10 by 6 feet by 16 feet 8 inches = 1,000 cubic feet. The total square feet of surface in the first room is 600; the total

SHIPPING ROOM OF RUSS BROS. OF HARRISBURG, PA.
Refrigerating machinery of this plant was equipped by the Frick Co., of
Waynesboro, Pa.

BUNKER ROOM FOR AIR COOLING — FAN INSIDE — DRIVE OUTSIDE.
Equipped by Frick Company of Waynesboro, Pa.

square feet of surface in the second room is 653; therefore, for the same cubical contents, the second room has 8.8 per cent. more radiating surface and will require 8.8 per cent. more material in construction.

The cold storage room should be where it is protected as much as possible from the direct rays of the sun. Unless some natural protection is afforded, such as trees or buildings, the cold storage room should be in the northeast corner of the building.

In the construction of a new plant advantage should be taken of the actual condition surrounding the proposed building site. Very often considerable may be gained by proper location of the building and arrangement of machinery.

One of the largest and most progressive firms making refrigerating and ice-making machinery is the Frick Co., of Waynesboro, Pa. Plants of all accepted types from the smallest to the largest, including all the latest improved methods that have proven, by test, to be worthy of adoption, are manufactured by this firm. This company has been making machinery for over thirty-two years with an enormous success.

IDEAL PLANT OF WHEAT'S ICE CREAM CO.

Like spotless town, like anything you have ever dreamed of in the way of sanitation and purity, is the new plant of Wheat Ice Cream Company, Buffalo, N. Y. Cleanliness is the watchword of this plant, and this feature was ever in mind when the building was constructed.

The company has its own ice plant, which produces 80 tons of ice daily. An ice storage room, which will hold approximately 500 tons of ice, guards the company against danger of shortage during the summer months.

Six gas engines supply the power for the compressors and electric generators, and every device to insure the safety of the employees while working on the machinery has been installed.

The employees are furnished with neat sanitary locker rooms, and a laundry in connection with the plant washes soiled clothing. In the plant everyone wears a white uniform.

The horses used in making deliveries are well cared for, in a separate part of the building. The entire stable is well ventilated.

The company also has a laboratory regularly furnished as a bacteriological laboratory, specially furnished as a laboratory for dairy products, and in charge of an eminent pure-food expert widely known in ice cream and dairy circles.

One of the departments worth noticing is the spacious milk refrigerating room. In the cooling vault hundreds of cans of pure lacteal fluid are given a dry, clean and sweet refrigeration. Another worthy innovation is the extract and fruit storage room, where whole luscious strawberries and other fruit in their original state are kept in crocks of ice, sugar and water. The temperature in this room is way below the zero mark.

The source of the refrigerating system is marvelous with its 12 miles of pipe through which ammonia flows. The building itself is as near fireproof as modern architecture will make it. It is reinforced concrete. The greater part of the walls are of white enameled brick, and all the floors

FREEZING ROOM OF THE WHEAT'S ICE CREAM COMPANY.

and walls can be flushed with hot water and steam. The
rooms devoted to the manufacture of the products are constructed so that dust and draughts from the outside cannot
enter. The mechanical equipment of the factory is perfect,
and throughout the entire process of manufacture the hands
of the employees do not come into contact with the product.
Visitors are always welcome to this plant.

IMPERIAL ICE CREAM COMPANY'S NEW PLANT AT PARKERSBURG, W. VA.

The arrangement of this new plant was worked out jointly
by John R. Livezey and L. J. List of Philadelphia, the
former a contractor for cold storage insulation, and the
latter general manager of The Mechanical Refrigerating
Co., who have equipped a number of the representative ice
cream plants in the east. Mr. Livezey acted in a consulting
capacity, devoting his time especially to the design and
supervision of all the insulation, including hardening
rooms, cream storage, ice storage, etc., the actual work
being done by the Armstrong Cork Co. Mr. List worked
out the arrangement and mechanical equipment of the factory, the refrigerating and ice-making plant being installed
by his own concern, The Mechanical Refrigerating Co.
The architectural details and active supervision of building
construction were in the competent hands of Edward R.
Wood, a local architect. The result was a plant which met
all the expectations of the owners, and the following brief
description and accompanying illustrations give some idea
of the many good points incorporated in its construction.

The skeleton of building is steel and concrete, with hollow tile floors and brick walls. The brick is buff colored and combined with green glazed ornamental tile coping and panels makes a very attractive appearance. The building is three stories high with basement, with a court in the rear for loading and wagon space, covered with ventilating skylights, and separating the main building from small stable. This is shown on the first floor plan. The interior throughout is plastered with hard cement.

The office is purposely small as the executive offices of the company are at Parkersburg. However, with a mezzanine floor above the reception hall, there is ample space for all needs. A glance at the first floor plan at once impresses one as providing a generous shipping floor. The company accumulates here a large number of orders for the various trains as the time for each approaches, and the large space provided is a great convenience. The local business is handled principally at the rear of shipping floor, from the court. Here crushed ice and salt can be delivered directly into the tank wagons.

The cream storage adjoins this room, and will easily accommodate 175 cans on the floor. It has an overhead coil bunker and is perfectly dry and sweet at all times due to the natural circulation which this construction insures. Beyond the cream room, space has been left for enlarging it should occasion require.

The rear of the second floor is occupied by a 25-ton ice tank and an ice storage room with a capacity of 75 tons of ice. Ice is loosened from the 300-pound cans in which it is frozen, and lowered automatically into the ice storage. A small passing door is provided for feeding the crusher

FRONT AND SIDE VIEW OF THE IMPERIAL ICE CREAM CO.'S NEW
PLANT AT CLARKSBURG, W. VA.

direct from the ice storage, and there is absolutely no chance of accident with the crusher. Immediately behind the ice storage room and above the point of use, the salt bin is located.

The third floor is devoted to storage, with a supply and stock room under lock and key, in addition to the large open space necessary for tubs, cans, cabinets, sidewalk signs, etc. The company does a large business in supplies, such as fruits, cones, ice cream boxes, grape juice, etc., running this as a jobbing department. There is no mechanical equipment on this floor, except the power for freight and bucket salt elevators, but immediately above the ice tank a cold water tank is located from which the ice cans are filled.

The basement accommodates the power plant and refrigerating equipment, both of which are of ample capacity and are designed to meet varied requirements. Power is supplied by two 165-h.p. Foos four cylinder gas engines using natural gas. These engines are arranged parallel with the west wall of building, set as far apart as possible, and connected by a shaft through flexible couplings. This shaft can be separated in the center by clutch couplings. On one side of this clutch coupling a 45-ton Vilter refrigerating machine is driven by belting direct, and on the other side a 35-ton Vilter refrigerating machine, a 75-kw. Westinghouse generator, a water pump and a brine pump are driven by belting direct. With two engine units of equal capacity arranged in this manner, either engine or either compressor can be operated in case of trouble with the other, as the compressor drives have a friction clutch on the shaft.

The generator is 3 phase A. C., same as the outside service which is connected for emergency use. The refrigerating machines are cross connected in such a manner that the work can be divided up in any way that is an advantage, and they are also provided with a safety attachment absolutely preventing any accident due to excessive pressures. In the front of basement is a locker room with shower bath, toilets, etc., for employees.

The brine tank and brine cooler which supply freezers are also located in the basement, close to the elevator shaft. The brine defrosting tank, motor driven pump and connections for defrosting the coils in the hardening rooms is located at rear of basement as is also the natural gas boiler which supplies the building with low pressure steam and hot water.

The description of the plant would not be complete without mention of the water cooling tower and ammonia condenser. These are immediately above the platform at rear of court, the condensers being at second floor level and water cooling tower starting at the third floor level. Returned empties are unloaded on the platform at the rear of the court and immediately next to the can-washing equipment. The shipping business is handled from the side of building. At the front of this floor is the freezing room, which is flooded with light and well ventilated by 10 large windows, all of which are screened.

There are six Tyson horizontal freezers now in place and provision for accommodating six more. The ice cream is passed from the freezing room through a small door to a gravity conveyor, from which it is placed in one of the four hardening rooms. The floor of freezing room is pitched to the rear of freezers where ample drainage is provided.

MIXING ROOM — FRONT OF SECOND FLOOR.

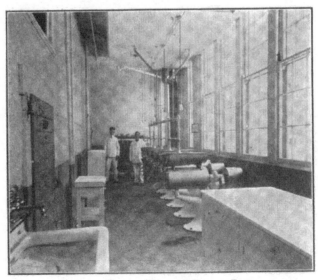

FREEZING ROOM — FRONT OF GROUND FLOOR.

One of the Pair of Four Cylinder Gas Engines in Basement.

The blast system hardening rooms are entirely independent of each other, having separate bunkers with 2-inch ammonia coils supported in baffles for deflecting the air which is circulated by a motor-driven Ventura fan, there being a fan for each room. Provision is made for circulating the air in the vestibules from the bunkers of the hardening rooms proper, thus keeping the vestibules at any desired temperature and free from frost and moisture.

The dipping room adjoining vestibule towards shipping floor is used for dipping any small orders, for preparing fancy forms and for the storage of fruits, etc. The entire room is refrigerated from an overhead coil bunker, and the room is always dry and cold from the natural circulation maintained. The cabinets are formed by steel tanks with steel tops through which cans are inserted and held rigid by special brass can clips. These cabinets are well insulated and provided with heavy insulated, counter-weighed tops.

Salt is supplied by a chute from large bin on the second floor, this bin being filled by a bucket conveyor fed direct from the wagon as it unloads from the car, through a hopper just below the first floor. The location of conveyor, hopper for unloading and supply spout are shown on the first floor plan.

Ice is fed from storage on the second floor, through a crusher suspended in the floor, and can be delivered into the bin on shipping floor or into tank wagons loading in the rear court, as desired. The ice bin is pitched to the rear and drained, and heavy perforated steel plates cover the bottom.

The can washing equipment consists of rinse tank, spindle washer and Fort Atkinson Sterilizer, all furnished by the Creamery Package Mfg. Co. Cans are stacked on trucks made of galvanized wire mesh and angle iron, and conveyed to the freezing room through a passageway behind the hardening rooms.

On the second floor, immediately above one end of the freezing room, a laboratory is partitioned off, and the balance of space across front of building is occupied by two 300-gallon Tyson mixers set in a rectangular depression to a convenient height, a Progress homogenizer, tubular cooler, and two batch pasteurizers, with a roomy dump platform immediately adjoining the elevator. The cream is brought up on the elevator to this platform from the shipping floor as received, the platform being just at a convenient height for dumping into the batch pasteurizers.

The water required for the ammonia condensers and gas engines is used over and over again by pumping up to the cooling tower, which is Burhorn. The condensers are of atmospheric type, made of extra heavy wrought iron pipe with sweated and soldered joints, and consist of 10 stands 18 pipes high and 20 feet long. The liquid receiver for same is suspended on the ceiling of the first floor above the passageway back of the hardening rooms.

The entire plant is up to the minute in all details and has proven economical and highly satisfactory in actual operation. With the opportunity of covering a wide and profitable territory such as Clarksburg affords through being a large shipping center, this plant should certainly justify the large investment and realize the expectations of its owners.

COMPRESSORS — LOCATED BETWEEN THE GAS ENGINES.

THE NEW MODERN PLANT OF TELLING'S BROS., CLEVELAND, OHIO.

THE FUTURE OF ICE CREAM MAKING IN THE SOUTH ILLUSTRATED IN AN ATLANTA PLANT

That the ice-making industry is interested in the development of the ice cream habit in the South is a foregone conclusion, for it furnishes a steady market for the product: but recently the industry has indicated a more direct interest in the increasing demand for this delicious frozen dainty. In other words, many of the ice manufacturers who are not inclined to " put all of their eggs in one basket " believe that the ice and ice cream combination is the simplest solution of their trade expansion problem, both from a mechanical and commercial standpoint. As a result, we note a more general adoption of the idea.

The city of Atlanta, the metropolis of the South, is successfully encouraging manufacturing enterprise. Naturally, the ice and refrigerating industry, the importance and extent of which is advancing steadily in every section of the South, is well represented. This is particularly true of ice cream-making plants, several modern factories having been erected in the last five years. Among these is the electrically-operated plant of Jessup & Antrim Ice Cream Co., on Ellis street, which has just been completed.

This company was organized about six years ago and installed the standard equipment of·that time, which answered the trade requirements until a year or two ago, when the owners decided to abandon obsolete methods and prepare for the growth in demand for ice cream. They visited the Refrigeration Exposition in Chicago for the purpose of selecting suitable machinery, and after careful inspection of the various exhibits awarded contract to The Triumph Ice Machine Co., of Cincinnati, Ohio, for a complete new plant, with capacity of 2,000 gallons of ice cream per day and daily ice capacity of 24 tons, the equipment being operated entirely by central station electric current. The ice cream-making machinery was furnished by the Tyson Co., of Canton, Ohio, and consists of three modern brine freezers, operated from shaft, and appurtenances.

The several photographic views of the plant accompanying this article furnish an excellent idea of the superiority of the plant as a whole, but they are not as perfect as might be desired owing to the fact that the equipment is located in the basement and the photographer found it difficult to get satisfactory views on this account.

The main building, shown in Fig. 1, is 40 x 100 feet, two stories and basement. Its construction and appearance are in harmony with the general character and surroundings of the plant, which, being located adjacent to a prominent residence section, are substantial and first class. Every precaution has been taken for the elimination of waste and danger of infection. The stables are far removed from the plant, being at the extreme rear of the lot, and are modern and sanitary in every respect. Provision is made for the care of fifty head of horses. The top of this building has been ingeniously utilized for the foundation of a water-cooling tower, and thereby the company has economized in the use of valuable real estate.

The refrigerating machines and piping system are shown in the foreground of Fig. 2, as well as in the floor plan of basement, the installation comprising two Triumph horizontal double-acting machines, one 9 in. by 18 in. and the other 12 in. by 20 in., both driven by Triumph a. c. motors of 220 volts. Observing closely, the reader will note a por-

tion of the ice tank, which contains 224 400-lb. cans, equipped with a Triumph shell brine cooler.

Without question, the most interesting part of this plant is the ice cream hardening rooms, a partial view of one of which is shown in Fig. 4. The still-air dry hardening system, on the flooded principle, is used, and provision is made for defrosting coils with hot gas from one of the ammonia compressors, the gas being available at all times by reason of the regular operation of one or the other machines. It is, therefore, practicable to accomplish this necessary work with the minimum of labor, without shutting down the plant, another advantage in the use of duplicate rooms.

The cream is introduced into the hardening rooms through revolving doors placed in close proximity to the freezers, a view of which is shown, which also illustrates the freezing room and defrosting connections, located in the rear of the hardening rooms.

Due to the rapid and efficient distribution of the refrigerant in the flooded system and the excellence of the insulating material used, the company has found it possible to maintain the required temperature with small loss by operating the plant on half time. A short run in the morning reduces the temperature to the required degree.

Manager F. E. Scanling states that since the plant has been in operation they have experienced no difficulty whatever in maintaining a temperature of 10 degrees below zero, and on several occasions it has been reduced to 20 degrees, at which point the temperature could be held regularly if desired.

Formerly it was considered advisable to use direct expansion piping for shelves in ice cream hardening rooms, but in this instance, for hygienic purposes, the shelves are made removable and no pipe is used in the rooms, except in the overhead bunkers.

A large ice storage room, in which a low temperature is maintained, as well as a sweet cream room, is located on the floor above the hardening rooms, the ice being elevated from the basement by means of elevating machinery manufactured by Warner Elevator Co.

A Creasey ice crusher is located on the same floor and adjoining the storage room entrance. By the use of galvanized downspouts, operated by gravity, delivery wagons may be filled with crushed ice by a single operation, or the ice sent to the ice bins in the packing rooms.

The management maintains a very liberal attitude toward the public with reference to inspection of the plant. Visitors, particularly local ice cream consumers and dealers, are cordially welcomed. Ice manufacturers and others, who are interested in modern ice cream-making methods, should certainly avail themselves of the opportunity to inspect this modern factory, which is a liberal education within itself.

The company is composed of the following members: A. Wesley Antrim, R. C. Jessup, Wilson S. Doan and Manager Scanling.

ICE MAKING

The manufacture of ice has developed into a profitable business for some of those engaged in it. It has even become a necessity in all the warmer localities. It is now

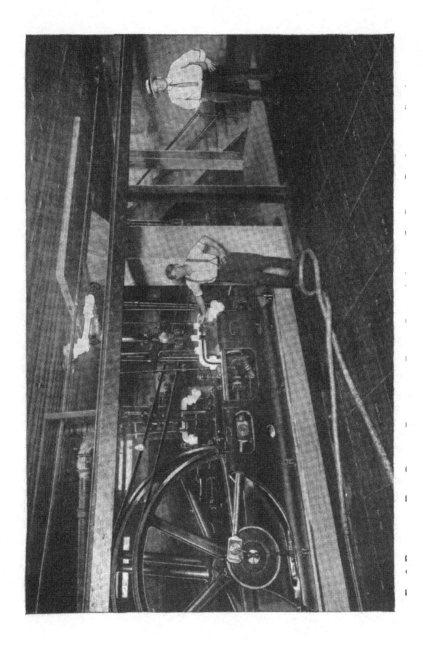

not so much a question of whether manufactured ice can be made at a cost low enough to compete with natural ice but rather, whether the natural ice obtainable in nearly all localities, is pure and fit for household use. The owners of ice-making plants in towns where only natural ice was used previously, find in some cases the public will demand or use artificial ice in preference to natural ice, chiefly on account of the natural ice being taken from ponds, streams and other sources, the purity of which is questioned. The only exception to this rule is the ice taken from large fresh water lakes located in the high mountain levels where there is little chance of contamination by anything dangerous to public health. In every case, manufactured ice meets the requirements of health boards and physicians. The ice is greatly purified in the process of freezing and distilled water, or comparatively soft water, filtered by means of the latest improved methods as adopted by hospitals and the like.

EXPENSE OF MANUFACTURE OF ICE

The operating expenses of an ice plant of a given capacity can be predetermined, as all expenses connected with the factory are fixed quantities for given rates of production. It is in every sense a routine business with no greater contingencies than, and as susceptible of exact calculation as, the business of pumping a given quantity of water.

The more extensive or greater the capacity of plant, the less cost per ton of production, but even plants of a daily capacity of a few tons prove remunerative investments.

Aside from the influence of the capacity of a plant, the cost of making ice also varies slightly in different localities, being affected by cost of fuel and labor. The difference is so little, however, that we find ice manufactured and sold in the South quite as cheaply as natural ice in the Northern cities.

It is a matter of congratulation that the machine-made ice has supplanted natural ice wherever introduced. It may not be generally known, but it is a fact, nevertheless, that manufactured ice will last longer than natural ice, owing to its density, absence of air, and low temperature at which it is frozen.

The operating expenses of a factory are made up of cost of fuel, light, oil and waste, slight loss of chemicals, sundry small repairs, salary of superintendent and engineer, with wages of firemen, tankmen and other labor. It is a paying investment to employ good men and best fuel obtainable.

ESTIMATED COSTS OF MAKING ICE — DISTILLED WATER CAN PLANTS

Tons Ice Daily	Engineers		Oilers		Firemen		Tankmen		Laborers		Bituminous Coal		Oil, Lights, sundries	Total expense daily	Expense per ton ice
	No.	Cost	No.	Cost	No.	Cost	No.	Cost	No.	Cost	Pounds	Cost			
3	2	$3 50									2,100	$2 90	$0 80	$7 20	$2 40
4	2	4 00									2,700	3 70	90	8 60	2 15
5	2	4 30									3,000	4 10	1 00	9 40	1 88
6	2	4 00									3,200	4 30	1 20	9 90	1 65
8	2	4 40					1	$1 80			3,500	4 70	1 30	11 70	1 47
10	2	4 20					1	2 00			3,900	5 30	1 40	13 00	1 30
12	2	4 20					2	2 20			4,300	5 70	1 70	14 00	1 17
15	2	4 80					2	3 60			5,300	7 00	1 90	16 50	1 10
20	2	5 00			1	$2 00	2	3 60			6,800	9 10	2 10	20 10	1 01
25	2	5 40			2	4 40	2	4 40			8,300	11 10	2 40	23 80	96
30	2	5 70			2	4 00	2	4 40			9,800	13 20	3 00	27 40	92
40	2	6 00			2	4 40	3	6 90			12,600	16 90	3 50	34 40	85
50	2	6 40			2	4 80	3	7 50			15,000	20 10	3 40	38 40	77
60	2	6 50			2	5 20	4	10 00			18,000	24 10	4 00	45 60	76
75	2	7 00									22,000	29 50	4 80	55 20	74
100	2	7 00							1	$2 50	27,500	36 80	6 00	70 00	70

Coal taken at $3.00 per gross ton delivered, which is a fair average.
To the above should be added 7 per cent to 3 per cent, depending on the size of plant and grade of machinery installed, for depreciation. Also about 3 per cent on cheap buildings and 2 per cent on good ones for depreciation.
Taxes and insurance form the balance of estimate of cost.
The estimates given are believed to be liberal for present conditions.
The above table is taken from Frick Company.

LUBRICATION OF REFRIGERATING MACHINERY

This is an important subject, and some users of machinery think that a cheap, low grade of oil is really cheapest. To disabuse their minds of this idea and suggest the necessity of high-grade oils, on the score of economy, and to keep the machinery at all times in efficient running order, is our object.

First-class refrigerating machinery calls for the use of three different grades of oil — Nos. 1, 2 and 3 — each of high quality.

No. 1. For Use in the Steam Cylinder, is known to the trade as *cylinder oil*. This ranges in price from 80 cents to $1 per gallon. Good cylinder oil should be free from grit, not gum up the valves and cylinder, should not evaporate quickly on being subjected to heat of the steam, and when cylinder head is removed a good test is to notice the appearance of the wearing surfaces. They should appear well coated with lubricant, which, upon application of clean waste, will not show a gummy deposit or blacken. Use this oil in a sight-feed cylinder lubricator with regular feed, drop by drop.

No. 2. For Use on All Bearing and Wearing Surfaces of Machine Proper. An oil which will not gum, not too limpid, with good body, free from grit or acid, and of good wearing quality, flowing freely from the oil cups at a fine adjustment without clogging; a heavier grade should be used for lubricating the larger bearings.

No. 3. For Use in Compressor Pumps. This oil should be what is called a cold test, or zero, oil of best quality. This oil, when subjected to a low temperature, should not freeze.

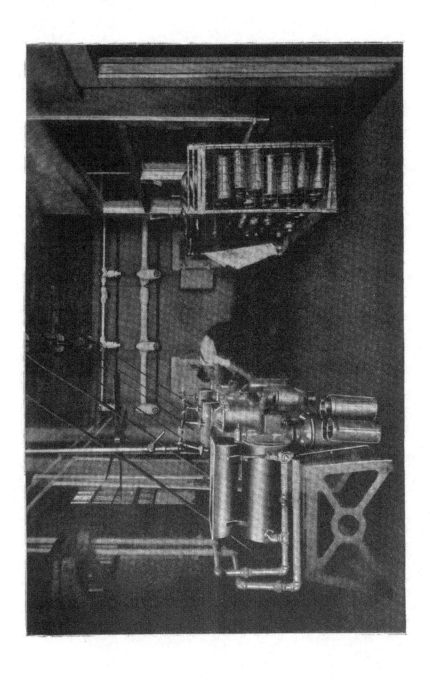

ICE-MAKING CAPACITY

This is dependent upon the temperature of the water to be frozen, and may be calculated as follows:

One pound of ice in melting into water at 32 degrees will absorb 143.5 positive units of heat; hence, it follows that water at 32 degrees will require 143.5 negative units to convert it into ice.

If the water to be frozen be taken from the usual source of supply — for instance, a pond or a river — its temperature in mid-summer may be as high as 92 degrees. This must first be reduced to 32 degrees before freezing commences; hence, 92 degrees, minus 32 degrees, equals 60 degrees, plus 143.5 degrees, which equals 203.5 heat units per pound of water frozen.

Manufactured ice is generally far below 32 degrees, because the temperature of the bath in which it is made ranges at about 20 degrees below the freezing point, and this work is to be added also. Taking into calculation the specific heat of ice, this extra negative heat would equal approximately 10 units, thus: $10 + 203.5 = 213.5$ hence

$$\frac{143.5 \times 100}{213.5} = 67.2 \text{ per cent.}$$ tons of ice made per re-

frigerating capacity. This is approximate, and does not take into account certain other items, such as losses by ice tank, can exposure, wastage in thawing out of molds, etc.

Time Required to Freeze Ice.
Can System.

Size of cans	Weight of cakes	Time to freeze
6 inches by 24 inches.............................	50 pounds.........	20 hours
8 inches by 32 inches.............................	100 pounds.........	36 hours
8 inches by 40 inches.............................	150 pounds.........	36 hours
11 inches by 32 inches.............................	200 pounds.........	55 hours
11 inches by 44 inches.............................	300 pounds.........	60 hours
11 inches by 57 inches.............................	400 pounds.........	60 hours

Note.— Temperatures of both, 14 degrees to 18 degrees Fahr. As rule, the higher the temperature the slower the process of freezing, but the finer and clearer the ice.

COLD STORAGE ROOM INSULATION

Refrigeration must be produced originally by a power plant; the ice machine must be driven by steam or electricity and these cost money every day. Hence it has been necessary to devise some means of cutting out this external heat so as to reduce the duty and cost of the refrigerating machine to a minimum. The modern means of preventing this entrance of heat is called insulation.

Builders of refrigerating machinery particularly voice the wisdom of using the best insulation. They know that their machines cannot make a fair record or satisfy the buyer if in addition to the legitimate and estimated task of refrigeration, they must struggle with unreasonable quantities of heat stealing in every minute and every hour through poor insulation.

In designing a room for storing ice cream the owner should consider with the utmost seriousness the kind of insulation material to be placed on the walls, ceiling and floor, because with good insulation the owner gets nearly as possible the full value of his refrigerating machines or his ice

MACHINE ROOM OF THE HOEFLER ICE CREAM CO., BUFFALO, N. Y., EQUIPPED
BY WEGNER MACHINE CO.

MACHINE ROOM OF I. N. HAGAN'S SONS PLANT OF UNIONTOWN, PA., EQUIPPED
BY THE WEGNER MACHINE CO.

in cooling his goods, and does not throw away his money cooling the air and ground in the neighborhood of his plant. Ice and refrigeration cost money continually every day and every hour, but good insulation costs only once.

Good insulation results in economies so vast that if the facts are brought home to him no reasonable man will hesitate to use it; it permits economies everywhere; a smaller refrigerating machine will do the work; less piping is required; in case of accident to the machines superior insulation will hold the temperatures until repairs can be made, and, by saving valuable stores from injury, may in a single emergency repay entirely its first cost.

The insulating material in a cold storage is more necessary than the refrigerating machinery. Before it is possible to carry water it is necessary to have a receptacle to hold it. Before it is possible to cool goods or to cool the temperature of a room it is necessary to have a receptacle like insulation to prevent the enormous ocean of heat out of doors from flowing into the cooled space as fast as the heat is removed by the refrigerating machinery.

A well-known refrigerating engineer has said: "Insulation should be considered in the light of a permanent investment, just as buildings and equipment, the returns of which should be based on the savings effected by the lower operating cost. It is a great deal cheaper to prevent heat from entering a building than to remove it by means of refrigeration."

By conduction is meant the transference of heat waves from one molecule or particle of matter to another. For instance, put one end of a poker in the fire and soon the other end will get hot, although far removed from the source of heat. This is exactly the process that goes on in the walls of a refrigeration or cold storage room. The outside is heated by the sun's rays or the warm air. The molecules on the surface are first set in motion. Gradually the vibratory movement spreads and goes deeper and deeper into the wall. When the molecular excitement gets into the insulation it travels forward less rapidly. The progress of the heat is impeded, just as piling along the water front breaks the force of the incoming waves. Still some of the heat eventually passes through, the amount depending upon the efficiency of the insulation. Slowly but surely the temperature of the room rises, unless refrigeration is continuously applied to offset the heat leakage.

The heat conductivity of dense substances — metals, whose molecules are heavy and close together — is very high; the conductivity of lighter material, such as wood, is less, while that of the gases is extremely low. Hence, air the most available gas is the most efficient insulator that can be had, if a vacuum, impracticable on the large scale, be excepted. But the problem is to confine it so that it cannot circulate; for the transmission of heat is also effected by other means called convection, or in other words, carrying of heat from one point or object to another by means of some outside agent, such as air or water, or any gas or fluid. Convection is the principle utilized in the ordinary house furnace. The outside air is drawn in through a duct, is heated and rises through pipes to various rooms, its place being taken by a new supply of cold, heavy air, which passes through the same process.

On a miniature scale this is exactly what takes place in every form of insulation. The side next to the outer air is

LIFTER ICE CREAM COMPANY OF PHILADELPHIA, PA., EQUIPPED BY YORK MANUFACTURING COMPANY OF YORK, PA.

warmer than the side next to the cold room. The air against the outer wall of each air space in the insulation becomes heated and rises, its place being taken by the cold air from the other side. As this becomes warm it forces its way upward; the other part, having gradually cooled, drops to the bottom, and thus a constant circulation is set up inside the air space itself. This movement tends to equalize the temperature on both sides of the air space and will continue as long as there is any difference in temperature. The fewer the air spaces the more rapidly will heat pass from one side of insulation to the other. Therefore the best insulation is that which embodies the greatest number of the smallest possible air spaces, for the smaller the air spaces the less extensive will be the effect of the circulation of the air confined therein. The problem is then, so far as the nonconduction of heat is concerned, to find some material which contains a large amount of entrapped air absolutely confined in minute particles.

To meet the demands of modern cold storage construction, however, suitable insulating material has to possess a number of other qualifications besides being an excellent nonconductor of heat. The plant owner demands that the insulation he installs retain efficiency indefinitely. This is merely another way of saying that it must not absorb moisture, for water is a good conductor of heat, and any insulating material that will absorb it will in a short time become worthless.

CORK INSULATION

Cork insulation has proven to answer all the requirements necessary and is used extensively and very successfully. Many years ago, the merits of granulated cork as an insulating material were generally recognized, but it was not until about fifteen years since, that widening knowledge of the demand for cork insulation in sheet or board form. To satisfy this demand some firms put on the market with great success cork pressed in blocks, sheets and boards.

WATER-PROOF LITH INSULATION

Water-proof lith is a standard insulation accepted by the profession of refrigerating engineering and indorsed in the most significant way, that is by continuous use, by several of the largest purchasers of insulation in the United States.

The substances used in the manufacture of water-proof lith are flax fibres, limestone rock, wool and water-proofing compound.

SODA FOUNTAIN SECTION

The soda fountain trade is still in its infancy. The opportunities of the business are beyond conception. It is estimated that the annual retail sales of soda fountain products in the United States now aggregate some sixty millions of dollars, and while these figures are large and interesting they are but a fraction of what may be expected within the next few years.

The soda fountain is the mecca for all classes and ages. With the rapid spread of the prohibition movement and the increasing number of new and seductive drinks, and above all, the growing enterprise of soda fountain dispensers, the increasing revenue to be derived from the sale of soda water drinks are enormously increased. It is a constant source of gratification to all who are engaged in the business of supplying temperance drinks that the soda fountain, while a silent worker, has a beneficial effect on the morals and health of our people, and has a wholesome influence for better citizenship.

The most successful fountain owner of to-day is the man who occasionally stops and takes a good look around, or in other words, the one who will read and think. There's hundreds of schemes to boost up this kind of a business. Take for instance, good, clever window display cards, special fancy flavors, strong advertising, etc. How frequent we notice how some stores continue business for years and just making a modest income, and how they work night and day struggling to make their ends meet. And after all this time and experience they watch a competitor who has a store just across the street who gradually wins most all the trade.

Why should this apparent anomaly exist? Ask the first firm and the answer will be that they cannot explain it; they will venture the opinion that fate has been against them. Study the second firm and you will see where lies the power. To begin with, the second firm has one or more men who have the broad viewpoint, and, they have a few well-defined policies and modern ideas. We trust that some of the following formulas and practical schemes will help to some extent to greater and more profitable accomplishments.

SCHEMES FOR INCREASING THE FOUNTAIN TRADE
BARGAIN DAY AT THE FOUNTAIN

In an endeavor to increase the sales of its soda fountains, the Owl Drug Co., a retail chain-store corporation operating drug stores in a number of Pacific Coast cities, recently offered one dollar coupon books containing twenty five-cent soda checks for fifty cents.

The offer was for one day only; and the five Owl stores in Los Angeles are reported to have disposed of 12,000 books, and to have turned away 6,000 would-be purchasers after they ran out of books. The coupons were good at any time, and the special luncheon service of the soda fountains was emphasized in the advertising.

OPENING DAY SCHEME

The proprietors of a soda fountain in a Western city occupied a full page in the local Sunday papers to advertise a grand opening of their soda fountain. The center of the page contained a fine cut of the fountain with this announcement underneath:

This is OUR NEW $5,000 FOUNTAIN, the finest in the city. To introduce this magnificent new soda fountain to the people of Blankville, the management has decided on the following program for the opening days:

On Monday the fountain will be in charge of the ladies of the First Methodist Church, and the management will donate to their building fund one-half of the day's receipts.

On Tuesday, a committee from the Masonic Orphan's Home will be in charge, and will receive one-half of all the receipts for that day.

On Wednesday the fountain will be run for the benefit of the Benevolent Orphan's Home, and that institution will receive one-half of the day's sales.

The management cordially invites the people of Blankville to call and see the new fountain during the opening days, and incidentally to assist the worthy institutions mentioned above by their patronage.

On the other side of this announcement was a list of drinks enticing enough to awaken thirst in a wooden Indian. — *Exchange.*

FREE TICKETS TO MOTION PICTURE SHOWS

There is no question about the hold moving pictures have on the public. One progressive fountain owner realized this fact and he made arrangements with the manager of a nickleodeon, near his store, to purchase tickets at a reduced rate. He then advertised free tickets with every ten cent ice cream soda. This scheme was worked on special days that were usually quiet. However, it brought fine results.

MENU CARDS AT THE FOUNTAIN

There are a great many ways in which a fountain proprietor can appeal to the public. One is by means of menu cards. They are, all things considered, the cheapest things a soda man can buy, and the more liberal he is in using them the better results will he obtain. The dispenser who is not using them is missing a valuable asset, as they have a hundred good points to every bad one.

Menu cards permit him to push his profitable drinks and sidetrack his unprofitable ones.

Menu cards allow him to serve twice the number of customers on a busy day, because he does not have to wait for their orders.

Menu cards permit any one, even a child, to take orders, leaving the manipulating to a responsible person.

Menu cards should not be expensive nor too elaborate. They should be so cheap that the druggist can afford to throw them away when they are even slightly soiled.

Menu cards should have on them a large blank space which should be headed " Special To-day." Under this heading the proprietor should push his more profitable drinks.

Menu cards should be changed frequently. If the house does not employ a capable dispenser let the druggist mix up the new drinks himself, show the boys how it is done, list them on the menu card, and see that the dispensers do the rest.

Menu cards are popular and will give a store the reputation of being up to date. The man who uses them will constantly hear his customers making such gratifying remarks as " He is always getting up something new.''

Menu cards permit one to push anything with which he finds himself overstocked.

If the druggist is selling ice cream soda for 5 cents, he may say on his menu cards, " Ice Cream Soda, 5 cents; Double Portion of Ice Cream, 10 cents; Sundaes, 5 cents.'' This will educate the public to the fact that there is a difference between a 5-cent soda and a 10-cent soda, and when he gets a call for a 10-cent one, he makes it up so good as to show a marked superiority over the cheaper kind, and before he knows it, he will be having calls for 10-cent ice cream sodas right along. Of course this applies only to districts in which 5-cent sodas and sundaes already prevail. In such localities, as a rule, the soda men are not very enthusiastic about their business, but just run it in a sort of don't-care way; if some one comes in and calls for a certain drink, he gets it or he doesn't and that ends the matter.

Menu cards advertise a fountain. Other things are advertised in your store, so why not the fountain?

Menu cards should be supplemented by advertising in papers and in the windows. When the menu is changed, let the other advertising be changed accordingly. If this plan is followed consistently it will pay.

ADVERTISING SUGGESTIONS

There are other reasons besides location to account for the crowds at Dean's fountain — try the soda! — Dean's, Los Angeles, Cal.

Refresh yourself during the summer days at our fountain. The delicious drinks with pure fruit flavors. Our pineapple, vanilla, chocolate and others are the best of their kind.— Hazelwood Co., Spokane, Wash.

The soda water we serve is sure to please those who appreciate quality.— Wanamaker, New York City.

Leave your thirst at our fountain. "The parting will be sweet."— Wanamaker, New York City.

The soda water we serve touches the thirsty spot and satisfies the fastidious ones.— Macy's, New York, N. Y.

A glass of soda smooths things out and ends lovers' quarrels, makes mamma and the children happy and braces up father for his business duties. There is nothing so refreshing or so bracing on a warm day as a glass of our ice cream soda made from pure fruit juices or our orange phosphate. Try it.— Smith, Lexington, Ky.

Our soda fountain is the chilliest, coldest, frostiest proposition in town.— Loranger & Culver, Saginaw, Mich.

A bargain in every glass. Some soda water is good and some is not so good. Ours is too good to sell for 5c, but as we cannot afford to sell a poor glass of soda any more than we can a poor drug, we will give you a bargain in every glass.— Jay Smith, Saginaw, Mich.

Dean's soda water is sure to please those who appreciate quality.— Dean's, Los Angeles, Cal.

PIECE OF ICE ON COUNTER A TRADE WINNER

Some dealers place a large pan on the counter or in a prominent place near the fountain, into which they place a large piece of ice. On top of this they cut a hole into which they set a punch bowl full of some kind of tempting fruit or whipped cream. This arrangement will also work for a window display.

———

PRACTICAL FORMULAS FOR BOOSTING THE FOUNTAIN TRADE

BANANA SPLIT

There are several ways of making banana splits, many of the dealers use several of the most convenient fruits which they have on hand. However, the idea is as follows:

Cut a banana through the center, that is length-wise, and place in oblong dish designed special for this purpose. Then take a dipper of ice cream and place on top of banana slices, and then pour over cream, berries, nuts, whipped cream and top off with a maraschino cherry. Banana splits should be made in proportion to the amount of money they are sold for, that is to say, use more or less fruit, nuts, etc., as to realize a reasonable profit.

———

PRINCESS SUNDAE

On a small plate arrange two No. 20 cone dippers of ice cream and two cones of water ice. Cover one with crushed peaches, one with a few slices of banana, one with chopped nut meats, and the other with whipped cream.

DREAMLAND SUNDAE

On a small platter put a No. 16 dipper of vanilla ice cream and one of water ice. Cover the water ice with crushed pineapple, cream with crushed cherries, these sprinkled with chopped meats; put a ladle of whipped cream between the cones and drop a cherry into it.

WILD STRAWBERRY

Shave ice, two-thirds glass; wild strawberry syrup, two ounces; orange cider, two ounces; sweet cream, one-half ounce. Fill with carbonated water and stir gently. Serve with straws.

WALNUT SUNDAE

Make a regular sundae with crushed pineapple and top with a spoonful of whole walnut meats or nut frappe.

SUNNET SUNDAE

A ladle of ice cream in a sundae cup. Pour over it a thin grape syrup; top with whipped cream and a fresh strawberry.

CHOCOLATE DIP

Split two lady fingers and place two of the halves parallel to each other on a fancy plate. On top of the two pieces and at the right angles to them lay the other two halves.

Add one ladleful of chocolate ice cream covered with chocolate syrup. Serve with whipped cream and top with maraschino.

PEANUT PARFAIT

Place a layer of vanilla ice cream in a narrow parfait glass, then a ladle of salted peanuts, then a layer of ice cream to fill the glass. Two kinds of ice cream may be used if desired.

WHITE PLUSH

Into a mixing glass place the white of one egg, one-half ounce of catawba syrup. Put into a tumbler half full of shaved ice and fill with milk. Shake thoroughly. Now place a spoonful of whipped cream in a tall mineral glass and strain the egg mixture into it; hold the glass high, and pouring in a long stream from one glass to the other. Serve with a spoon.

FLOWING STREAM

Into a mixing glass one-third full of shaved ice, pour one ounce of catawba syrup, one-half ounce of orgeta syrup, and fill up with milk. Shake well and strain into a tall, thin glass. Top with nutmeg and serve.

SNOWDRIFT SURPRISE

In a sundae glass or cup place a ladle of prepared grated cocoanut. Over this pour a ladle of heavy chocolate syrup, so that the cocoanut is covered completely. The confection now looks dark, but when you dig into it with a spoon the " snowdrift " appears. A delightful confection, and something out of the beaten track. Cocoanut is becoming popular and may be served in numerous ways.

ORANGE ICE PISTACHIO SUNDAE

Ten to quart dipper orange ice, ladleful of crushed pineapple. Cover with whipped cream and on top of the whipped cream sprinkle liberally with half meats of green pistachio nuts.

ORANGE ICE FRAPPE SUNDAE

Turn a ten to quart dipper of orange ice into a sundae cup. Peel and separate into quarters an orange; place three sections at equal distances around the side of the sundae, top with whipped cream and surmount with a cherry.

ORANGE ICE CHOCOLATE SUNDAE

Use an oblong banana royal dish. On one side put a size sixteen round measure of chocolate ice cream and on the other side some of orange water ice. Pour chocolate sauce over both, sprinkle with ground walnuts and cover liberally with whipped cream.

ORANGE SURPRISE SUNDAE

Take a full round slice of pineapple that has been cored. Lay in a sundae dish, put a maraschino cherry in the hole, add a size twelve dipper of orange ice, cover the whole thing with whipped cream and sprinkle the top of the whipped cream with broken filbert nuts.

CHERRIFIED ORANGE ICE SUNDAE

A size ten dipper of orange water ice, over this pour three or four maraschino cherries with their liquor and powder with ground walnuts.

GRAPE COOLER

Grape juice, one ounce; raspberry syrup, one-half ounce; orange syrup, one-half ounce; lime juice, one teaspoonful. Mix well with some shaved ice and fill glass with carbonated water. Decorate with a cherry.

GRAPE LEMONADE

Make an ordinary seltzer lemonade and float one ounce of grape juice at the top. No handsomer or more refreshing drink than this one.

GRAPE GLACIER

Serve in a mineral tumbler or tall, narrow glass. Fill glass nearly to the top with shaved ice and pour as much grape juice in the glass as it will hold. This is a splendid way to serve grape juice.

ORANGE ICE PHOSPHATE

Draw into a soda glass an ounce and a half of orange syrup, add a sixteen to quart measure of the orange ice, a dash of phosphate, and fill with plain soda. This will make an intensely cold drink.

ORANGE SALAD SUNDAE

On a small oblong dish place two lettuce leaves. On each place a No. 16 dipper of vanilla ice cream. Over one pour sliced orange fruit. Over the other fresh crushed strawberries. Top each with whipped cream and a cherry.

GRAPE FLOAT

Put a No. 10 cone dipper of vanilla ice cream into a sundae cup, and pour over it one-half ounce of ice cold grape juice. Then sprinkle with chopped walnuts or other chopped meats, and crown with a maraschino cherry.

PINEAPPLE A LA DELMONICO

Place a slice of pineapple on a fancy plate and place a fancy mould of ice cream, resembling some fruit, such as an apple, peach, pear, etc. Place two lady fingers on either side of the plate or a couple of slices of nice fancy cake.

PINEAPPLE IMPERIAL

Any flavor. The pineapple imperials are made same as the plain pineapple sundae, only using fancy ice cream, which may be made in any flavor that you have.

PINEAPPLE GLACE

Place a slice of pineapple on a dish and on it a No. 10 cone dipper of pineapple water ice, and top with a maraschino cherry. Other glaces may be prepared from any flavor of water ice or sherbet that you carry, naming the glace after the flavor of the ice. Thus, if you use raspberry water ice it should be called " Raspberry Glace."

WHIPPED CREAM

Whipped cream is prepared by beating cream stiff with an egg beater or cream whipper. Cream thus prepared is used in the preparation of many fancy beverages and for topping both cold and hot drinks.

The cream purchased for whipping must be rich and heavy. Usually the cream for this purpose contains from 40 to 45 per cent. of butter fat, and should be at least 24 hours old as cream. Cream containing as low as 25 per cent. of butter fat, if sufficiently aged, will whip, and therefore the heavy cream may be mixed with milk in the proportion of one part of milk to two parts of cream and still whip nicely. However, when cream thus diluted and whipped stands for any length of time the milk separates and falls to the bottom and is lost.

Some use sweetened whipped cream, and for use with cold drinks this is preferable. For this purpose a little sugar or syrup may be used. It may also be sweetened with a little vanilla syrup — a sweetening that will be found to be best adapted for use at the average fountain. The vanilla must be the very best and should not be too pronounced, only a mild flavor being desired.

Cream that is intended for whipping should be thoroughly chilled in order to secure the very best results. Some add a little gelatine solution to give body to the cream; this is especially desirable when the cream is to be used for making charlotte russe, etc., where the cream must be made to stand up for some time.

Another method is to skim the froth from the cream while whipping, using 25 per cent. cream. This gives a lighter or more frothy product and makes the .cream go farther, but will not give the same satisfaction that the heavy product does. To each pint of chilled cream used add the usual amount of sweetening and two ounces of gelatine solution (one ounce dissolved in two pints of water) and whip slowly for a minute or two until a heavy froth gathers on top. Skim off the froth and put in a suitable container for counter use, and then continue the process until you have frothed all the cream that will froth or whip.

Some add the white of eggs to cream when whipping it. Use the whites of three eggs to each pint of cream if you do this. If you want something really nice nothing equals the plain cream with a little sweetening.

Whipped cream must be kept cold in order to preserve it in real good condition. A bowl set in shaved ice makes the best container.

———

MILK SHAKES

Milk shakes consist of milk sweetened with some flavored syrup and shaken thoroughly with a little fine ice to thoroughly chill and foam it. If it is desired to do away with the fine ice then the milk must be chilled until it is ice cold before using, otherwise it will not whip up and give the richness that makes a milk shake so delicious.

The proper glass for a milk shake is a 12-ounce glass. Into your glass draw from one and one-half to two ounces of the desired syrup, add your fine ice and fill three-quarters full with milk and shake thoroughly, then strain into a clean glass.

The shaking should foam the drink so that it will fill the glass. The principal flavors called for are vanilla, chocolate, coffee and fruit flavors. Milk shakes should bring ten cents, although in some sections of the country they are still sold for five cents.

All milk drinks not topped with whipped cream may be sprinkled with either cinnamon or nutmeg if the customer desires.

———

PHILADELPHIA SHAKES

These are prepared in the same manner as the milk shake, only you use one-half cream and one-half milk in place of all milk. They may be made in any flavor and should bring fifteen cents.

11

CREAM SHAKES

These are prepared the same as milk shakes, only all light cream is used, and they are usually served in a 10-ounce glass, and should bring from twenty to twenty-five cents each. Philadelphia shakes are sometimes called '' Cream Shakes.''

FROZEN CREAM SHAKES

This may be flavored with any desired syrup. Into a mixing glass draw one and one-half ounces of the desired syrup, add four ounces of sweet cream and one-third glass of very fine ice, fill nearly full of milk and shake thoroughly. Pour without straining into a 12-ounce glass and float a No. 16 mound of vanilla ice cream on top.

SPLITS (ANY FLAVOR)

These are very fine; chocolate and coffee are the flavors to push. They are called from the name of the syrup as '' Chocolate Splits.'' Into a 7 or 8-ounce glass draw one ounce of the desired syrup and add a small ladle of whipped cream, fill with milk and stir with a spoon to mix the syrup with the milk, being careful not to mix the cream, but leave it to float on top.

BETSY MOORE SUNDAE

Put a No. 10 cone of vanilla ice cream into a sundae cup and pour over it a ladle of coffee marshmallow dressing. Sprinkle with chopped nut meats and top with a maraschino cherry.

HEAVENLY DREAM SUNDAE

Cut a fully ripe and thoroughly chilled cantaloupe in half and remove the seeds. Put one of the halves in a suitable dish. Pour a little crushed pineapple in the bottom of the cavity. Put a No. 12 scoop of maple ice cream in the melon and pour over it a ladle of fruit salad. Vanilla ice cream can be used if you do not have the maple. Top with whipped cream and a cherry. The following makes an excellent fruit salad for this purpose: Remove the pits from a pound of black ox-heart cherries. Peel and separate into sections three oranges. Peel three bananas, chop the cherries, slice the bananas and oranges, mix together and cover with sugar overnight. In the morning add one-half pint of crushed pineapple.

BLACK AND WHITE SUNDAE

On a split banana put a No. 16 cone of chocolate ice cream and a No. 16 cone of vanilla ice cream. Over the vanilla pour some crushed pineapple and cover with whipped cream. Over the chocolate pour some chop suey dressing and some chocolate marshmallow dressing and sprinkle with nut meats. If desired, the other can be sprinkled with flaked cocoanut.

STATE HOUSE SUNDAE

Put a No. 12 mound of coffee or chocolate ice cream in the center of a small plate. On this put a No. 20 cone of vanilla ice cream and pour over it a ladle of rose marshmallow.

CANADIAN SPECIAL

In the center of a small plate put a square slice of fruit cake. On this place a No. 10 cone of strawberry ice cream. Over this pour a ladle of marshmallow cream dressing and sprinkle with chopped pecans. Top with whipped cream and decorate with whole fresh strawberries. When not in season use cherries.

FRUIT SALAD DRESSING

Mix one and one-half quarts of fresh crushed strawberries with one and one-half quarts of fresh crushed pineapple. Add one quart of crushed cherries. Broken maraschino cherries can be used and one quart (two pounds of such fruit as dates, figs, citron, etc., chopped). Reduce to a good dispensing consistency with simple syrup.

COFFEE SHAKE

Coffee syrup, two ounces; milk, four ounces. Add shaved ice and shake thoroughly. Fill glass with plain soda, using fine stream moderately. A drink popular with coffee lovers, although some will not want quite so much syrup. A good coffee drink will win trade that will stick to you through thick and thin, for the true coffee lover thinks no coffee so good as his own favorite brand.

ALASKA SNOW BALL

Lemon syrup, one-half ounce; orange syrup, one-half ounce; cream, one ounce; eggs, two; shaved ice, sufficient.

Mix the eggs, cream and syrups in the glass, put in ice to fill latter three-fourths, shake the whole thoroughly, strain into a 12-ounce glass, almost fill the latter with the coarse stream of carbonated water, and top it with powdered nutmeg.

FROSTED GLACE

Into a mixing glass two-thirds full of shaved ice put two dashes of solution of acid phosphate, one and one-half ounces of claret syrup and one-half ounce of pineapple syrup. Fill the glass nearly full of carbonated water, stir thoroughly, then take a fancy glass, put into it a large tea-spoonful of frozen fruit sorbet, having previously dipped the rim of the glass in water and then in powdered sugar. This gives the glass a frosty appearance. Finally strain the contents of the mixing glass into the fancy glass and serve.

GRAPE SUNDAE MALTED

Put a No. 10 cone of vanilla ice cream in a sundae cup and pour over it one and one-half ounces of Concord grape juice and sprinkle with malted milk. Decorate with Concord grapes and when out of market use Malaga grapes. This is especially nice for those who want something that is not sweet.

WHITE AND YELLOW SUNDAE

On a banana split dish place a sixteen to quart measure of vanilla ice cream and a sixteen to quart of orange water ice. Pour a ladleful of crushed pineapple equally over both,

sprinkle on the top some chopped black walnut meats, place
between the two a liberal spoonful of whipped cream and a
maraschino cherry on the top of that, and serve with a
spoon and a side drink of ice water. This sells for fifteen
cents.

ISLAND SUNDAE

Place a slice of pineapple in a dish and on it a No. 8 cone
of ice cream. Pour over it a little orgeat syrup and sprinkle
with chopped nut meats. Top with a cherry.

SUMMER SCHOOL

_nto a sundae cup place a cone of vanilla ice cream and
cover with one ladleful of chocolate syrup and one ladleful
of chopped nuts. Put one green and two red cherries on
each side and sprinkle over all one teaspoonful of malted
milk.

YANKEE SUNDAE

Put a No. 8 dipper of ice cream in a champagne glass and
cut a hole in the center of the cream with a spoon, and fill
it with crushed strawberries; dress with whole cherries and
cut pineapple, and serve lady fingers or sweet wafers.

CREAM EGG SHAKE

Into a 14-ounce glass break one egg, add two ounces of
wild cherry syrup or a sufficient quantity of milk and shaved
ice. Shake well, fill with carbonated water, course stream.

CHOCOLATE ALMOND SUNDAE

Place a portion of vanilla ice cream in a glass, pour over it about one ounce of chocolate syrup (or a little more if desired) and sprinkle with chopped almonds. Both the syrup and the ice cream may be varied.

CLUB SANDWICH SUNDAE

Place a slice of vanilla ice cream on a dish, place over this two sweet wafers, and over them a slice of chocolate ice cream, giving a perfect sandwich. This sandwich is sometimes served on a lettuce leaf. Chopped nuts and fruits may also be used for filler; likewise sliced orange (relieved of its rind) and other sliced fruits if desired. Sliced banana answers the purpose well, as it may be eaten easily with a spoon. If you have a sandwich mold made you can get elaborate effects.

BEAUTY SUNDAE

Place in a sundae dish a measure of strawberry ice cream and cover with crushed pineapple. Place three cherries around the side and top with whipped cream and chopped nuts.

CHOCOLATE DAINTY SUNDAE

Put a No. 10 cone of vanilla ice cream into a sundae cup and pour over it a ladle of chocolate cream dressing, then top with whipped cream and decorate with a chocolate cream drop.

CHOCOLATE BANANA SUNDAE

On a split banana place two No. 20 cones of chocolate ice cream. Over one pour a ladle of chocolate walnut dressing. The other with bitter sweet chocolate dressing. On the top of each cone put a dab of chocolate marshmallow dressing and a little bitter sweet chocolate drop.

THREE-IN-ONE SUNDAE

Take a No. 10 disher and fill it with three kinds of ice cream, chocolate, strawberry and vanilla, and put it into a sundae cup. Over this pour a little of three kinds of fruit and top with a nut, fig and a cherry.

ROSE BUD SUNDAE

Put a No. 10 cone of vanilla ice cream into a sundae cup and pour over it a small ladle of crushed maraschino cherries. Over this pour a ladle of American beauty dressing. Sprinkle chopped walnut meats about the base of the cone. Top with a dab of whipped cream. This may be decorated either with a few candied rose leaves or a cherry if you do not have the other.

A MIDSUMMER NIGHT'S DREAM SUNDAE

The following formula will make from three quarts to a gallon of delicious fruit syrup to pour over a sundae, adding whipped cream and cherry to top off:

6 bananas, cut fine and mash.

4 oranges, cut fine and mash.

1 quart strawberry syrup.
1 quart raspberry syrup.
Mix well together.
It is a dream.

FRUIT SALAD SUNDAE

A dainty sundae served in a fancy footed sundae glass is of strawberry ice cream, crushed pineapple fruit, crushed cherries, fancy whole nuts, sliced orange, shredded fig. Top off with whipped cream and whole cherry. Sell for fifteen cents.

NORTH POLE SUNDAE

Serve in six-ounce low parfait glass. Use about one-half glass of pulp peach fruit and one-half glass lemon sherbet. A very small amount of vanilla ice cream can be used around the edges of the glass to resemble snow. Insert a candy opera stick in the center of the glass. Cover over with whipped cream and use a cherry to finish the top of the pole. Sells for twenty cents.

SWEET SIXTEEN

Put a No. 10 cone of vanilla ice cream in a champagne glass. On this put four " festino " almonds and pour over it a ladle of maple walnut dressing. Decorate with whipped cream and four cherries.

PEACHES AND CREAM SUNDAE

On a small platter put three small lettuce leaves. On the center one put a No. 10 cone of vanilla ice cream. Peel, remove stone from a large, ripe peach and cut in half. Slice each half on one of the other lettuce leaves. Sprinkle with powdered sugar and cover with whipped cream. Cover the ice cream with rose marshmallow dressing and top with a cherry. This can be varied by using pistachio marshmallow dressing and topping with a green cherry.

SIAMESE TWINS

Place a red banana split lengthwise in an oblong dish and on it put two No. 16 cones of chocolate ice cream. Over each one pour a little chop suey dressing and top each one with some chocolate marshmallow dressing.

OPERA SUNDAE

Put a No. 10 cone of vanilla ice cream into a sundae cup and pour over it a ladle of crushed peaches, sprinkle with chopped nuts, cover with whipped cream and decorate with several slices of fresh peaches.

FRUITED CREME DE MENTHE SALAD

Place two small lettuce leaves on a suitable dish. Put a No. 20 mound of vanilla ice cream on each. Cover one with fruit salad. Cover the other with mixed nuts. Dress both with whipped cream and top with a cherry. Serve a small pitcher of creme de menthe syrup on the side.

———

CANADIAN FAVORITE

Put a No. 10 cone of ice cream in a sundae cup. Sprinkle with chopped nut meats. Place four cherries at the base and one at the top of the cone.

———

TEXAS GIRL SUNDAE

Put a No. 10 mound of vanilla ice cream in a champagne glass. Sprinkle with chopped pecan nut meats. Pour over it a little cherry syrup and decorate by placing four cherries around the base of the mound and placing a marshmallow on top.

———

NEW YORK CANTALOUPE SUNDAE

Place a lettuce leaf in a sundae cup and then place a portion of cantaloupe on it. Put a No. 16 mound of vanilla ice cream into the cantaloupe and top with a maraschino cherry.

———

NEAPOLITAN NUT SUNDAE

On a six-inch plate place a slice of neapolitan ice cream, and on it place a No. 16 cone of vanilla ice cream. Over this pour a little of crushed pineapple, then sprinkle with chopped nut meats and top with whipped cream.

MILADY SUNDAE

At one end of a small platter place a No. 10 cone of vanilla ice cream. At the other end place four lady fingers side by side. Over the lady fingers pour a ladle of fresh crushed strawberry and cover with a ladle of whipped cream. Over the ice cream pour a ladle of fresh crushed strawberries and top with a maraschino cherry.

———

CANTALOUPE JOY

Put a portion of cantaloupe in a sundae cup and in it place a mound of vanilla ice cream, and cover with crushed pineapple.

———

CANTALOUPE NUT NOVELTY

Put a portion of cantaloupe in a sundae cup and place in it a mound of coffee ice cream. Top with whipped cream and sprinkle with chopped nut meats.

———

BRIGHTON SUNDAE

This is another name that is given to a Cantaloupe Joy.

———

KING GEORGE CANTALOUPE

Place a portion of cantaloupe in a sundae cup and put a No. 16 cone of vanilla ice cream in the center. Over the cream pour a small quantity of fruit salad dressing. Place two or three pieces of pineapple on the sides of the cone, and top with a maraschino cherry.

SURPRISE SUNDAE

Put a No. 16 cone of chocolate ice cream in a parafait glass. Take a spoon and push the cream into the bottom of the glass in such a way as to make a hollow in the center. Over this pour a ladle of crushed pineapple and drop two maraschino cherries into it. Nearly fill the glass with vanilla ice cream, pour over it a ladle of marshmallow creme dressing, and top with a spoonful of chopped nut meats and a cherry.

VARIETY SUNDAE

On a rather large sundae dish place a portion of vanilla ice cream, making with the spoon as many depressions in the same as there are crushed fruits to be served with it. In each depression pour a small ladleful of crushed fruit, a different kind in each. Garnish with whole fruit and be sure to charge enough to pay for the confection and the time consumed in preparing it.

SEASHORE SUNDAE

Into a dish put four ounces of crushed cherries, add an equal quantity of figs cut in small pieces, also of dates stoned and cut in the same manner. Reduce to a working consistency with cherry syrup. When serving top with whipped cream and a cherry.

MALLO-CREME SUNDAE

A portion of ice cream; serve as a " topping " Mallo-Creme, plain or with any kind of fountain syrup, fruit or chopped nuts. This also applies to buffaloes, Bostons, etc.

MALLO-SCOTCH SUNDAE

A portion of vanilla ice cream; top with Mallo-Creme and Mallo-Scotch Sundae, prepared as per direction No. 4. Sprinkle with nuts if desired.

COCOA MALT SYRUP

Malt extract, eight ounces; vanilla extract, one dram; orange syrup, two ounces; cinnamon syrup, two ounces; wine cocoa, two ounces; simple syrup, eighteen ounces. Serve still in an eight ounce, or with foam, in a twelve ounce-glass as desired. They may also be served with phosphate if desired.

GINGER MALT SYRUP

Extract of malt, thick, two ounces; soluble extract of ginger, four drams; lemon syrup made from the fresh fruit, two pints. Serve still in an eight-ounce glass with or without phosphate.

SLICED ORANGE NUT SUNDAE

Place a portion of ice cream in a sherbet glass. Over this pour a small amount of orange syrup. On each side of the ice cream place slices of orange. Over all a serving of Mallo-Creme. Top with chopped walnuts.

ROAST ALMOND SPECIAL

Put a No. 10 mound of vanilla ice cream in a sundae cup and pour over it a ladle of fresh crushed strawberries.

Sprinkle with crushed roasted almonds, cover with whipped cream and top with a cherry.

_____

NUT BAMBOO SUNDAE

Put a No. 10 mound of vanilla ice cream in a sundae cup and pour over it a ladle of dressing made by adding shredded cocoanut and chopped nut meats to chocolate syrup. Top with whipped cream and decorate with stuffed dates and a cherry. The stuffed dates are prepared by removing the pits and putting nut meat in the place of them and then rolling in powdered sugar.

_____

BASE BALL SPECIAL

Slice half a banana in thin slices into a fruit nappy and pour over it a ladle of fresh crushed strawberries and put a ladle of whipped cream on top. Take a No. 16 round disher and fill it heaping and rounded full so that when dropped into the whipped cream it will resemble a ball. Serve a clover leaf wafer on the side of the dish.

_____

RED PINE PHOSPHATE

Draw one ounce of pineapple syrup and one ounce of blood orange syrup into a ten-ounce glass, add a couple of dashes of acid phosphate and fill up with plain soda, mixing with a spoon.

_____

SNOWBALL SUNDAE

Put a No. 12 scoop of ice cream rounded full so as to represent a ball into a sundae cup and pour over it a ladle of snowball dressing.

SNOWBALL DRESSING

To one-half gallon of regular maple marshmallow cream dressing add one quart of chopped Hawaiian pineapple, one quarter pound flaked cocoanut, one-quarter pound of chopped walnuts and the same of pecan nut meats, and then mix thoroughly.

BONNE BELL CREAM

Pineapple syrup, three-fourths ounce; vanilla syrup, three-fourths ounce; ice cream, two ounces; egg, one; shaved or cracked ice, one-fourth soda glassful. Shake in a shaker, or glass and shaker, strain into a twelve-ounce glass, nearly fill the latter with the coarse stream of carbonated water and " finish " with the fine stream.

BISQUE CREAM

Roasted almonds, four ounces; extract of vanilla, one-half dram; soda syrup, thirty-two ounces. Break up the almonds to coarse powder, boil for a few minutes with about eight ounces of the syrup, allow to cool, strain and add the extract and the remainder of the syrup. This is to be served in twelve-ounce glass with or without ice cream.

BLIZZARDINE

Orgeat syrup, one ounce; catawba syrup, one-half ounce; ice cream, one teaspoonful; shaved or cracked ice, one-half soda glassful. Shake together in a shaker, strain into a twelve-ounce glass, nearly fill the glass with the coarse cream of carbonated water and "finish" with the fine stream.

ELYSIAN PUNCH

Juice of half an orange; pineapple syrup, one-half ounce; grape juice, one ounce and a half. Add plenty of shaved ice and plain soda to fill glass. If not sweet enough, add a little powdered sugar to taste, or the amount of pineapple syrup may be increased. Garnish with sliced pineapple.

GINGER ALE GLACIER

Serve in a mineral tumbler, or tall, narrow glass. Fill glass nearly to the top with shaved ice and then pour in as much ginger ale as the glass will hold. A delightful way to serve ginger ale.

ORANGE JUICE FRAPPE

Break an egg and use the white only. By passing the yolk back and forth, one-half the shell to the other, the white will gradually drain off into a twelve-ounce soda tumbler. Beat this white of egg to a froth. Squeeze the juice of a good-sized orange into the same glass. (Be careful to remove the seeds.) Fill the glass with fine cracked ice, or better, shaved ice. Add one spoonful granulated sugar. Place in a shaker and shake well. Serve with a couple of straws. This is a very delicious, and at the same time, healthful and nourishing hot weather drink. Sells for ten cents.

12

SNOWBALL PARFAIT

Into a mixing glass put a No. 16 cone of lemon water ice (orange ice may be used if lemon is not at hand); a No. 12 cone of vanilla ice cream and a small quantity of crushed pineapple. Mix and transfer to a parfait glass and top with whipped cream. This may be served without any decorations or a candied violet may be dropped on top. Sells for fifteen cents.

THE PURPLE DEEP

Into a mixing glass draw one-half ounce of vin fiz syrup and three-quarters ounce of raspberry syrup. Add a little ice and fill one-half full with milk, shake and strain into a twelve-ounce glass and nearly fill with carbonated water, using the fine stream only. Cover with whipped cream, then carefully place a No. 16 mound of strawberry ice cream on top. Top with a cherry. Sells for ten cents.

DEVELOPER OF FLAVOR

Malo-creme when added to any flavored syrup while it dilutes it, nevertheless it so develops the flavor that it makes it much better for serving on ice cream than the straight syrup, and this quality makes it possible to use as a flavor for ice cream dressings, substances that would otherwise be too expensive to use.

MARSHMALLOW FRUIT SUNDAE

A great many varieties of fruit sundaes can be made by flavoring marshmallow whip with fruit syrups, pineapple, raspberry, strawberry, etc., as follows: Marshmallow whip, one pint fruit, syrup, two ounces. Mix thoroughly. Serve over vanilla or other ice creams.

MARSHMALLOW NUT SUNDAE

Marshmallow whip, one pint; ground pecan nuts, English walnuts, one ounce. Beat nuts through whip and serve over ice cream.

CHILL CHASER

Soluble fluid ginger, three ounces; infusion of gentian, twelve ounces; lemon juice, eight ounces; infusion of lemon peel (one to twenty), four ounces; water, twenty-one ounces; brown sugar, five pounds.

LIME SLIP

Into a twelve-ounce glass draw one ounce of pineapple syrup and one ounce of orange syrup. Into this squeeze the juice of one lime. Fill the glass one-third full of ice and the balance with carbonated water. Mix and decorate with slices of orange and pineapple.

NAPA ORANGE

Into a twelve-ounce glass draw one ounce of orange syrup, one ounce of raspberry syrup and squeeze in the juice of one lime. Fill the glass half full of lemon ice and the balance with carbonated water. Mix, decorate with cherries and serve with a spoon.

LIME JUICE FLIP

Into a twelve-ounce glass draw one and one-half ounces of lemon syrup and one-half ounce of lime juice; add three dashes of phosphate and a little ice. Into this break an egg and shake thoroughly. Fill with carbonated water and strain into a twelve-ounce glass.

NEWPORT COOLER

Into a twelve-ounce glass draw one and one-half ounces of ginger ale syrup and squeeze in the juice of one lime. Fill the glass one-third full of fine ice and the balance with carbonated water. Mix and decorate.

MAPLE NUT NOUGAT

On a small oblong dish place two No. 16 cones of vanilla ice cream. Pour over them a little maple syrup. Over one cone cut some maple nougat candy and sprinkle the other with chopped nut meats and top off with whipped cream.

YANKEE SUNDAE

Put a No. 10 mound of ice cream in a champagne glass and cover with fresh crushed strawberries. Over the top drop three cherries, four pineapple cubes or small cuts of Hawaiian pineapple, a section of orange and two whole strawberries. Serve three assorted wafers.

SUNSHINE SUNDAE

On a six-inch plate place No. 8 cone vanilla ice cream. Put four sunshine wafers on cone. Use pineapple and strawberry fruit and top off with whipped cream and cherry. Sells for fifteen cents.

CHOCOLATE NUT FREEZE

Put an ounce of chocolate dressing, a ladle of whipped cream or an ounce of heavy cream and a spoonful of chopped nut meats into a sundae cup and mix thoroughly. Make a ball of ice cream with a No. 12 mound scoop and drop it into the mixture.

BOSTON ICE CREAM SODA

This is the name generally given to ice cream sodas which also contain sweet cream. These are prepared by drawing the desired amount of syrup into the glass and adding from one-half to one ounce of sweet cream. Then fill about three-fourths full, using both the coarse and fine streams. Drop the portion of cream on top and then fill the glass by using the fine stream. With a little practice you can become so expert that you fill the glass just to the right point with soda, so that when the cream is added it will just fill the glass. Many fountains at which ice cream soda is served for five cents do a good business. In Boston ice cream sodas sell for ten cents.

In the far west one of the methods after putting the syrup and cream in the glass, is to fill them with the fine stream only. This certainly makes the very finest ice cream soda, although it does not give as large a quantity of drink as by the other method. For a ten-cent ice cream soda the usual size of glass is a fourteen ounce, using from two to two and one-half of syrup, and using an ice cream scoop giving ten or twelve portions to the quart. I have known some men to use a scoop giving only eight portions to the quart, but to our mind this is too much.

RAINBOW PHOSPHATE

Into a ten-ounce glass draw one-half ounce of each — raspberry, orange and pineapple syrup — and fill with carbonated water.

GINGER ALE RICKEY

Powdered sugar, one teaspoonful; juice of one lime. Add half a glass of shaved ice and fill tumbler with ginger ale.

CANTALOUPE A LA MODE

Divide a fine, ripe canteloupe in six sections lengthwise. Clean and remove seeds and soft part. In the hollow place a scoopful of vanilla ice cream. Dust with chopped nuts. Top the cream with a cherry.

CHOCOLATE NUT FREEZE

Take one quart of orange syrup, formula for which is given above, and two gallons of plain water, and one ounce of fruit acid solution. Mix well together and sweeten with sugar; if you wish sweeter, suit your taste. Color with orange color until it is a golden yellow. Put in iced orangeade dispenser and draw out an 8-ounce mineral glassful, garnish with a thin slice of orange and serve with a straw.

If you have calls for orangeade iced or think best to serve it iced to your trade, then you use a large 12-ounce soda glass and add a scoopful of shaved ice, and serve same as written above.

CREAM IN PLAIN SODA

Plain cream adds much to many soda flavors, but it makes a difference how it is used and how it is dispensed. Some use merely a dash or about a teaspoonful, some half an ounce, and some even an ounce. It is not well to use too much, but better use too much than too little and a half ounce is little enough; it may cost a little more to be liberal, but it will pay in the end.

Cream may be properly served with any flavor that is not acid, and even with acid flavors at the request of your customer, though they should not be recommended.

When serving such flavors as vanilla, coffee, chocolate, peach, etc., sweet cream should be used unless ice cream or no cream is specified by the customer.

The correct method for making is as follows: Draw the syrup in a 12-ounce glass, add one and one-half ounces plain cream. Use fine stream to thoroughly mix the cream with the syrup, then coarse stream and finish with fine stream.

NEVADA PARFAIT

Into a mixing glass put a portion of vanilla ice cream, a small quantity of whipped cream, one-fourth of an ounce of heavy chocolate syrup, such as is used for making hot chocolate, and mix thoroughly. The ice cream must be in good condition, otherwise the mixture will be too soft. Fill a parfait glass one-half full of this mixture and add a teaspoonful of chopped pecans. Convert them with a very thin layer of plain vanilla ice cream. Fill one-half of the balance with the mixture, add a few more chopped nuts, walnuts or hazel nuts, and then fill the glass with the mixture, placing a dab of whipped cream on the top. Serve with a spoon and a glass of plain soda on the side. This should be sold at twenty cents or at the very lowest fifteen cents. It will look nice and taste as good if you take pains with it.

CHERRY COLLEGE ICE SPECIAL

Put a No. 10 mound of vanilla ice cream in a sundae cup. Put a ring of six maraschino cherries around the edge. Cover with whipped cream and sprinkle with crushed roasted almonds.

COFFEE FRAPPE

To every quart of clear, good Mocha coffee add one pound of sugar, and freeze as directed above.

CHOCOLATE FRAPPE

Dissolve one pound of chocolate (powdered) with four quarts of water, adding two pounds of sugar, seeing that the chocolate is fully dissolved; remove from the fire and strain. When cold, flavor with vanilla and freeze after the manner laid down for frappe.

PINEAPPLE FRAPPE

Peel and crush two pineapples; then make a boiling syrup of two and one-half pounds of sugar and two quarts of water and pour it over the pineapples. Let stand until nearly cold, then add the juice of five lemons; pour into freezer, add four egg whites and freeze. Then work in a good half pint of maraschino.

LEMON FRAPPE

Make an ordinary lemon water ice; rich in fruit, flavor good and sweet; then freeze.

ORANGE FRAPPE

This is made on the same lines as the foregoing, substituting orange water ice.

For sherry frappe, add a pint of sherry wine to every quart of lemon water ice.

For claret frappe, add one pint of claret to every quart of orange water ice.

MATINEE SUNDAE

Put a No. 10 mound of strawberry ice cream into a sundae cup, pour over it a ladle of fresh crushed pineapple, top with whipped cream and decorate with a cherry.

OPERA DROP SUNDAE

Put a No. 10 mound of chocolate ice cream into a sundae cup and pour over it a ladle of chocolate nut dressing, then cover with whipped cream and drop into the whipped cream half a dozen chocolate opera drops.

ORIENTAL SUNDAE

Put a No. 10 cone of chocolate ice cream into a sundae cup and over it a ladle of chocolate almond syrup and top with a cherry.

BISMARCK SUNDAE

Put a No. 10 cone of vanilla ice cream into a sundae cup. Over this pour a ladle of date and fig dressing. Top with whipped cream and sprinkle with powdered cinnamon.

MARBLE CAKE SUNDAE

Place a slice of marble cake on a small platter. At one end place a No. 16 cone of chocolate and vanilla ice cream at the other, and with a decorating bag make cake cone of whipped cream in the center. This may be served plain, or a little maple syrup poured over the cream. Top with a cherry.

DELMONICO SUNDAE

For this sundae, use a long dish and put a small ladle of ice cream at each end. Then cut half of a banana into four thin slices lengthwise. Put two of the pieces on the dish in an outward V-shape between the two molds of ice cream; then place a slice of sweet orange around the entire dish in each of the vacant places, or four all told. Pour over this an ounce of cherry wine syrup and sprinkle with nuts; top off each mold with whipped cream and a cherry.

FRUIT SALAD FOR SUNDAES

Select one quart of strawberries that are sound and ripe, cut or chop them into two or three pieces, but do not crush, and add as much sugar as they will absorb. Peel a nice ripe pineapple, cut into small pieces and cover with sugar. When the sugar has absorbed all the juice, add the berries, and about the same amount of whole cherries, a quart of chopped fruit, such as dates and figs, citron, etc., and enough simple syrup to enable you to serve it nicely.

RAINBOW SUNDAE

On a small oblong glass dish place two small thin slices of peeled orange. On one put a No. 16 cone of strawberry ice cream. On the other a No. 16 cone of vanilla ice cream.

Over the vanilla ice cream pour some caramel dressing and sprinkle with chopped nut meats. Over the strawberry pour a ladle of marshmallow cream dressing and sprinkle with pistachio nuts. Between the cones put a ladle of whipped cream and sprinkle with shredded cocoanut and top with a red and green cherry.

NABISCO CREAM NUT SUNDAE

To one quart of cream add two and one-half pounds of sugar and almost bring to a boil, cool and add one-half pound of chopped pecan nut meats, one-half ounce of vanilla extract, and eight ounces of ground Hawaiian pineapple. Put a No. 10 cone of vanilla ice cream in a sundae cup. Place a nabisco wafer at each side of the cone and pour over it a ladle of the dressing.

SPECIAL CHOCOLATE SUNDAE

Put a No. 10 mound of chocolate ice cream in a sundae cup. Over this pour some chocolate dressing. Over this pour a ladle of whipped cream and spread it out so that it covers the mound completely. Drop half dozen little chocolate buds into the whipped cream and the same number of pecan halves.

PINEAPPLE MELBA

Place a slice of canned pineapple on a six-inch plate, a No. 8 cone of vanilla ice cream on top of pineapple, then spread crushed pineapple over the ice cream and top off with whipped cream and cherry. Sells for fifteen cents.

CHOCOLATE PECAN PUFF (A SUNDAE)

Put into a suitable glass one No. 10-to-the-quart ladleful of vanilla ice cream, and cover it with a mixture of one-half ounce chocolate syrup, 1 spoonful of whipped cream, and one-half ounce of pecans. The dressing should be prepared fresh as called for. Yields a good profit at fifteen cents. The author writes that this is a favorite with the " sorority girls " of his city.

MALLO-ROSE SUNDAE

Put into a suitable sundae dish a scoopful of strawberry ice cream and the same quantity of vanilla ice cream. Around the sides of the dish place a banana (sliced), and decorate with mallo-rose dressing and two large maraschino cherries. Mallo-rose dressing is made as follows: Mix two pints of marshmallow creme with 1 pint of simple syrup and color to a light red or pink with soluble rose, and then with this mix one-half pound of whole pecan nut meats. Serve with a sundae spoon.

FLAG DAY SUNDAE

Use a fancy sundae dish with foot. Into it put a No. 10-to-the-quart disherful of vanilla ice cream. Cover the cream with a ladleful of whipped cream and then sprinkle on some assorted gum drops. In the center of the mixture stick a small flag. Arrange the gum drops in the order of the colors — " red, white and blue." Sells for fifteen cents. The flag is given to the customer as a souvenir. The author

states that this sundae is suitable for the Fourth of July,
Labor Day, or can be used on the occasion of any patriotic
celebration.

HAPPY JACK SUNDAE

Into a twelve-ounce glass put a sliced banana, and on it
put a No. 20 disherful of ice cream. Sift on some powdered
or broken nut meats, cover with marshmallow dressing,
slightly stir, and serve with a spoon.

BABY DOLL SUNDAE

Into a saucer or small plate put a large scoopful of vanilla
ice cream; around the cream place four nabisco wafers; between the wafers put some strawberries, fresh fruit, if it
can be gotten; then top with " baby doll dressing," made
as follows: Two bananas, 2 ounces crushed pecans, two
ounces crushed pineapple, and one ounce of whipped cream,
all well mixed together. Keep the dressing on ice and use
as wanted. The author gets twenty cents per dish for this
sundae, and writes that it is a good seller in his territory,
a Southern city.

GRAPE VINE SUNDAE

To one quart of grape juice add one cupful of sugar and
bring the mixture to a boil. Then add four heaping teaspoonfuls of cornstarch dissolved in water. Cool. To make
the sundae, place on a suitable dish one cone of ice cream,
cover with the " grape vine " dressing, add a teaspoonful

of whipped cream, which " spot " in the center with a fragment of crushed cherry. Place a slip of parsley on each side of the cherry.

COCOANUT BISQUE SUNDAE

Grind a pound of cocoanut crisp (candy) through a food chopper, using the coarse knife. This is the dressing. To make the sundae, take one cone of ice cream, any flavor, cover with whipped cream and dust heavily with the ground cocoanut prepared as above. Top with a " spot " of crushed cherry and decorate with parsley. The author states that one, if he so desires, can use almonds, filberts, or peanut crisp in place of cocoanut bisque. He writes: " It doesn't sound so fancy, but it *eats* fancy, and the *eat* gets the money."

7-11 SUNDAE

On a suitable sundae dish put a disherful of vanilla ice cream; over the cream put two ounces of 7-11 dressing, and place chocolate nabisco wafers around the sides of the dish; top off with a liberal supply of whipped cream. Sells for fifteen cents.

The dressing is made as follows: Thoroughly mix in an egg mixer, two ounces of chocolate syrup, one and one-half ounces of malted milk, and two ounces of sweet milk.

PANATELLA BREEZE (A SUNDAE)

In a large sundae dish place a No. 12-to-the-quart disherful of vanilla and strawberry ice cream, half-and-half. Over

this pour two ladlefuls of the following dressing: Marshmallow syrup, four ounces; chocolate syrup, one ounce;
ground pecans, two ounces; maraschino cherries, forty.
Mix well and use as a dressing. When placed on the ice
cream, top with a little whipped cream.

SILVER SUNDAE

Make a thin paste of marshmallow whip, which pour over
a cone of ice cream (No. 12-to-the-quart dipper); sprinkle
over with cocoanut, and top off with marshmallow. Sells
for 15 cents. The author of this formula writes: '' This
sundae has made a great hit with our trade and we give a
silver spoon with each dish.''

CHOCOLATE NOUGAT

Granulated sugar, one-half pound; chocolate, one-half
pound; milk, eight ounces; lemon juice, one-half ounce;
crushed pineapple, one can; nuts, six ounces. First mix the
milk, chocolate and sugar together, cook over a slow fire for
about five minutes, then slowly add the lemon juice and cook
until the mixture comes to a boil; add the nuts and crushed
pineapples, mix, and set aside to cool. To serve, place a
No. 12 scoopful of chocolate ice cream on a suitable dish,
cover with chocolate nougat, and top off with whipped cream
and a cherry. Sells for 15 cents.

NUGGET SUNDAE

Place a No. 12 cone of vanilla ice cream on a dish; put three whipped cream chocolates evenly around the bottom; pour maple syrup over the ice cream, sprinkle on a few ground nut meats and top off with whipped cream and a cherry. Sells for 15 cents.

––––––

EGG MALTED MILK

Vanilla syrup, two ounces; milk; one egg; malted milk, two heaping teaspoonfuls; cracked ice, a sufficient quantity. Draw the syrup into the glass, add the egg, cracked ice and malted milk. Shake until the egg is well beaten, then fill the shaker about one-third full of milk and shake again. Finally add milk enough to fill the shaker about two-thirds full; shake well and strain into a clean glass. Top off with a little powdered mace, nutmeg or cinnamon.

––––––

ROYAL EGG PHOSPHATE

Into a mixing glass put two ounces of cardinal syrup; one egg; solution of acid phosphate, 1 dash; vanilla ice cream, one teaspoonful, and enough carbonated water to fill the glass two-thirds full. Mix thoroughly with an electric shaker and top off with whipped cream and a cherry.

13

GINGER ALE COBBLER

Into a twelve-ounce glass squeeze the juice of one lime, and to it add one and one-half ounces of ginger ale syrup and one and one-half ounce of pineapple syrup. Put in about one-third glassful of finely shaved ice and fill the glass with carbonated water. Mix and decorate with a slice of pineapple and a maraschino cherry.

KINGSDALE FRUIT PUNCH

Strawberry syrup, ten ounces; orange syrup, 10 ounces; pineapple syrup, ten ounces; lemon juice, two ounces. Mix and use as a fruit syrup. To serve, fill a fourteen-ounce glass one-third full of shaved ice, put in one and one-half ounces of the syrup, and nearly fill with carbonated water; add a few strawberries, a slice of pineapple, a slice of orange, and serve with straws.

HUNGRY CLUB SANDWICH

On a banana-split dish put a banana cut lengthwise in two equal parts; on one end place a No. 16 disherful ·of vanilla ice cream, and on the other end a disherful of chocolate ice cream. Decorate with slices of sweet orange and cherries, and place a few fresh strawberries on the side. Cover lightly with ground nuts.

NECTAR FRUITY SYRUP

Pineapple syrup, eight ounces; raspberry syrup, eight ounces; orange syrup, four ounces; lemon syrup, four ounces; vanilla syrup, four ounces; morella cherry syrup, four ounces. Mix. Use as a stock syrup and keep on ice. To serve, place a small cone of vanilla ice cream in a fourteen-ounce glass, add one and one-half ounces of the nectar syrup, and fill the glass with carbonated water. The syrup can also be used as a covering for sundaes.

BRYAN PEACE NUT SUNDAE

Into a large sundae dish put a No. 10-to-the-quart disherful of vanilla ice cream. Around the ice cream place a ring of marshmallows, and above this a ring of six walnut halves. Add two red and two white or green cherries, and over all pour one ounce of grape juice. Serve with nabisco wafers.

ORANGE NUT SUNDAE

Into a sundae dish put a No. 10-to-the-quart disherful of vanilla ice cream, then add sliced orange, cut in diamond-shaped pieces, and sliced pineapple, cut in triangular shape; then cover with English walnut meats and maraschino cherries. Syrup may be used if desired.

SANITATION AT THE FOUNTAIN

The consumption of ice cream and soft drinks has increased so rapidly during the past few years that these commodities can no longer be regarded as luxuries, but must be considered as important articles of food.

In order that the purchaser may not be in doubt as to the character of the goods which he is buying, it is necessary that more attention be paid to the sanitary production of these articles of food. It is also necessary that more care be given to their proper labeling.

It may be that in the past insufficient emphasis has been

placed on these matters. It is with the intention of clearly stating our views on these matters in a form accessible to all that this book is issued.

DECOMPOSITION

The materials such as syrups, crushed fruits, cream, ice cream, etc., from which soft drinks, sodas and sundaes are made are subject to rapid deterioration. They readily spoil and therefore become unfit for food unless proper methods of preservation are used.

To intelligently handle these materials requires a knowledge of the causes of spoilage.

Decomposition or spoilage is, in most cases, due to some of three causes, molds, yeasts or bacteria.

Molds develop on substances containing sugars, starches or fruit acids. They injuriously affect the quality, flavor and food value of the substances which they attack and generally impart thereto a musty taste and odor. Moisture is necessary for their development.

Yeasts decompose the sugars present in fruit juices, syrups, etc., produce alcohol and give off a carbonic acid gas. Syrups which have been attacked by yeasts have a frothy appearance due to the rising of small bubbles of carbonic acid gas; they generally have a sour odor and are said to be fermenting.

Bacteria attack the nitrogenous materials at the fountain, such as nuts, milk and cream, and ice cream. They are the cause of putrefaction.

Most of the diseases of man are caused by bacteria. These bacteria multiply at an enormous rate during the progress of the disease. The disease producing bacteria are carried to other persons by means of their food and drink.

Molds, yeast and bacteria are everywhere present; in the air, in water and on food-stuffs. They are generally present in an inactive (" seed " known as spore) condition.

These spores (germ seeds) develop only where they find suitable conditions.

In general, the conditions under which yeasts, molds and bacteria grow most readily (and consequently spoilage takes place most rapidly) are presence of moisture (water), a warm temperature and absence of sunlight.

While the spores of molds, yeasts and bacteria are everywhere present about the fountain, the number in which they are present are in proportion to the amount of dust and dirt present.

Clean fountains are comparatively free from molds and bacteria. Dirty fountains harbor large numbers.

HARMFUL BACTERIA

From the standpoint of healthfulness, the kind of bacteria is of greater importance than the number.

Many bacteria are harmless to man when taken into his system. Others are the causes of tuberculosis, typhoid fever, diphtheria, summer complaint and other diseases. Harmful bacteria are carried to the fountain in milk, cream and ice cream supply from diseased employees; in the glasses and spoons used by diseased patrons; or are carried from filthy places by flies, cockroaches, rats, mice, dogs or cats.

FOUNTAIN AND EQUIPMENT

The fountain should be attractive but of simple construction. Many fountains are now on the market which permit of rapid and thorough cleaning. The old so-called " tombstones " are insanitary.

The floor behind the counter should be of cement, tile or other non-absorbent material. The floor should drain to a catch basin in the center.

Purchase plain glass and silverware. Dirt is easily removed from them. Decorated silver and rough glass surfaces are seldom clean. Much labor may be saved by purchasing only plain, smooth accessories.

Protect straws from dust, dirt and flies. Do not unnecessarily handle them.

The practice of placing straws in jars where children can play with them is decidedly insanitary. Frequently older persons are seen unconsciously playing with the straws so exposed.

There are many sanitary straw containers on the market which dispense but one straw at a time. By the use of these inexpensive machines, the customer is sure of having a clean straw to place in his mouth.

Never expose straws on the tables or counter where they may become filthy as a result of being handled.

Table tops and counters should be constructed of some material impervious to water. The varnish on wooden tables and counters soon becomes destroyed by the water used in keeping them clean. Where wooden tables are used the table may be kept in fairly good condition by a daily application of a mixture of one pint of benzine and one pint of paraffin oil.

DAILY CLEANING

The fountain should never be permitted to remain in a dirty condition during the night. The accumulation of refuse and slops is heavily loaded with molds, yeasts and bacteria. During the warm weather they grow very rapidly and many give off foul odors. These odors developing near the fountain contaminate the soda materials and spoil their flavors. Harmful disease producing bacteria also greatly increase in number if permitted to grow during the night. In a few hours a few bacteria may become many thousands.

At the close of the day's business, all glasses, spoons, drain boards, sinks, tables and counters should be carefully washed; the garbage pail removed and emptied; and the floor behind the counter scrubbed with hot water and washing powder.

Do not have anything behind or under the counter beneath which dirt and slops can accumulate. The drain boards, cooler boxes, cabinets, etc., should be so constructed as to have the floor beneath them accessible for scrubbing.

The foul odors noticed at many fountains are caused by the decomposition of the material carelessly permitted to remain under these furnishings.

A filthy floor under the counter is inexcusable.

The room should be well ventilated during the night.

ALL GLASSES, SPOONS, JARS, ETC., AND ALL DRAIN BOARDS, SINKS, TABLES AND COUNTERS SHALL AT ALL TIMES BE KEPT IN A CLEAN AND SANITARY CONDITION (see Section 2, Sanitary Food Law).

SIMPLE SYRUP

Purchase only the best grade of unblued granulated sugar for the preparation of simple syrup.

Use only pure water. There is absolutely no excuse for using dirty or impure water at the fountain.

If pure water is not obtainable from the city water supply, it may be rendered pure by distilling. Water can be distilled at a cost of one-half cent per gallon.

Water which contains no harmful bacteria but which is cloudy may be cleared by filtering. Filters which remove the greater number of bacteria from the water are obtainable but they work too slowly to be of service for obtaining water for the fountain.

Clean syrup is probably most easily made by means of a syrup percolator. The sugar and syrups are protected from dirt and dust in the percolator. Percolators should be frequently cleaned. The cloth strainer over the diaphragm should be removed and well washed with water (do not use soap). Boil the cloth in clean water and replace. The cloth used for straining simple syrups made by other methods should be similarly treated.

Simple syrup should be stored in clean bottles or jugs which have been sterilized with boiling water. Fill container full to the neck and stopper at once.

Do no use wooden containers for syrup.

Yeasts and molds cannot grow in heavy syrups. Make the simple syrup using at least twelve pounds of sugar to each gallon of water. If necessary, dilute when using.

SODA FOUNTAIN SYRUPS

SIMPLE SYRUP

To make simple syrup pour one-half gallon of boiling water on eight pounds of granulated sugar — this makes approximately one gallon of finished simple syrup. If desired you may add glucose which has a tendency to thicken it; this is not necessary; however, some dealers use it to some extent.

Many people use percolators in making simple syrup, which does away with the heating of the water and is simply used by placing sugar and water in the top and draining off by faucet near the bottom when syrup is desired. An apparatus of this kind proves efficiency where sugar is used extensively, as all the draining of sugar from barrels and bags can be used without any trouble.

VANILLA SYRUP

Simple syrup .... 1 gal.
Extract of vanilla, about..................... 2 ozs.
Soda foam .... 1 oz.
Color with a little caramel.

FLORIDA ORANGE SYRUP

Simple syrup .... 1 gal.
Extract orange .... 2½ ozs.
Fruit acid .... 1 oz.
Soda foam .... 1 oz.
Color with curcuma.

LEMON SYRUP

Simple syrup .... 1 gal.

Extract of lemon .... 2 ozs.

Soda foam .... 1 oz.

Fruit acid .... 1½ ozs.

Color with curcuma.

PEACH SYRUP

Simple syrup .... 1 gal.

Peach juice .... 1 pt.

Soda foam .... 1 oz.

Fruit acid .... 1 oz.

LEMON SYRUP FROM THE FRUIT

Select from eight to twelve fine, juicy lemons, according to the size. Grate eight of the twelve lemons, taking care to grate only the yellow part of the rind, into a good sized mortar or other suitable dish. To the gratings add eight ounces of sugar and rub thoroughly so that the sugar will absorb the oil. If necessary add more sugar so as to obtain all the flavor from the rind. Before rubbing with the sugar, some add half an ounce of alcohol to the gratings, believing that it cuts the oil and aids in extracting the flavor. This is optional; not at all necessary. When the sugar has been rubbed into the thing set it aside for a few hours; over night will be none too long if you can so arrange it. When you are ready to finish the syrup express the juice of the dozen lemons and strain over the gratings and sugar and stir until the sugar is dissolved; then strain through a double thickness of cheesecloth and add enough simple syrup to make one gallon of finished syrup. If desired, add one ounce of fruit acid.

GINGER ALE SYRUP

Simple syrup	1 gal.
Ginger ale extract	4 ozs.
Fruit acid	½ oz.
Caramel color	1 oz.
Soda foam	1 oz.

ALMOND SYRUP

Simple syrup	1 gal.
Extract bitter almond	1 oz.
Soda foam	1 oz.
Fruit acid	1 oz.

SARSAPARILLA SYRUP

Simple syrup	1 gal.
Extract sarsaparilla	1 oz.
Soda foam	1 oz.
Caramel to color	1 oz.

PEAR SYRUP

Simple syrup	1 gal.
Pear extract	2¼ ozs.
Soda foam	1 oz.
Fruit acid	1 oz.

CHOCOLATE SYRUP

Cocoa .... 8 ozs.
Granulated sugar .... 8 lbs.
Water .... 1 gal.
Vanilla extract .... 1 oz.

Mix the sugar very thoroughly with the cocoa while dry, then add hot or boiling water gradually, then place on stove until it starts to boil. Do not let it boil too much. Some dealers use a small portion of salt to chocolate to bring out the flavor. Use a double kettle for this kind of work.

CHOCOLATE SYRUP

Cocoa .... 8 ozs.
Sugar .... 10 lbs.
Water .... 3 qts.
Vanilla extract .... 1 oz.
Condensed milk .... 1 pt.

The above formula will be rather rich and heavy and will not keep very long. However, it is used by some soda dispensers. Mix in the same manner as the previous formula for chocolate syrup.

CHERRY FLIP SYRUP

Mix thoroughly one-half gallon of champagne syrup, one quart of cherry syrup, one quart simple syrup, two ounces fluid extract of wild cherry and one ounce of fruit acid.

CHERRY LACTART SYRUP

Mix thoroughly five pints of black cherry syrup, one pint of lemon syrup, one pint of orgeat syrup, four ounces of simple syrup, and twelve ounces of lactart.

MAPLE SYRUP

1 gallon of simple syrup.
2 ounces of maple extract.
Color with a little caramel.

CHERRY SYRUP

1 gallon simple syrup.
2 ounces cherry syrup.
Red color.
2 ounces citric acid solution.
1 ounce soda foam.

ROOT BEER SYRUP

1 gallon simple syrup.
1 ounce root beer syrup.
Caramel to color.
1 ounce soda foam.

STRAWBERRY SYRUP

3½ quarts simple syrup.
1 pint strawberry juice.
1 ounce fruit acid solution.
1 ounce soda foam.
Color red.

PINEAPPLE SYRUP

3½ quarts simple syrup.

1 pint pineapple juice.

1 ounce fruit acid solution.

1 ounce soda foam.

Color if desired.

VANILLIN vs. VANILLA BEANS

By the Late E. C. SPURGE, Niagara Falls, N. Y.

Modern science is always seeking to get at the why and wherefore of things. Does any natural product possess any marked properties as to odor, flavor or curative powers, then sooner or later, it will fall under the trained observation of the chemist who, by patient study and research, isolates and determines the bodies to which its peculiar properties are due. Practically all of nature's most valuable odors, flavors and remedies are produced in minute quantities hidden away in enormous and variable quantities of inert vegetable tissue and extractive.

Years ago when science was unequal to the task of isolating such bodies — the whole plant or parts of the plant were used. Later, extracts were made which were supposed to represent the extractive principles of the plant. These, although more convenient to use than the plants themselves, were not satisfactory, owing to the fact that the work of nature influenced by soil, climate conditions, etc., so that the quantities of active principle varies considerably and extracts made from a given weight of the plant would, therefore, not be uniform in strength. These disadvantages were manifest to the practical man, and led to the demand for a uniform product which would represent the active principles of the plant free from inert and useless vegetable matter. This practical need stimulated the efforts of scientists to isolate the active principles in a state of purity.

In case of the vanilla bean many attempts were made long ago to determine the aromatic principle to which it owed its delicate and characteristic odor. After a considerable amount of preliminary work by Vee, Gobly and other chemists, Messrs. Tiemann and Haarmann, after a prolonged investigation, succeeded in discovering its real identity and further showed that the bean contained practically no other flavoring principle. As vanilla beans only contain from ¾ to 2 per cent. of vanillin, the incentive to try the manufacture of it synthetically was very great, and Messrs. Tiemann and Haarmann made great efforts to effect the synthesis. They succeeded in manufacturing it first from the sap of pine trees, and then from guaiacol — a product obtained from beech tar. From these two sources the vanillin was comparatively expensive, and it was not until the method for its preparation from clove oil was discovered that the manufacture was begun on a large scale, about the year 1876.

The synthetic product was found to give such excellent results that it was at once received with great enthusiasm and the success of the product stimulated eager research into other flavoring principles and odors. Possibly it is not too much to say that the synthetic perfume industry dates from its discovery — at any rate, it gave it a great impetus. To-day the white, shining crystals of the product — 100 per cent. pure — form the best means of introducing the vanilla flavor into all kinds of confections, since they are of uniform strength, and faithfully represent the natural aroma and flavor of the bean. It may be admitted that an extract of the beans has a different odor than that of a solution of vanillin, but the aromatic resins giving this odor to the extract are comparatively feeble in flavoring value, and in the finished confections their influence is not noticeable, and only the vanillin remains.

Since vanilla beans will not contain more than ¾ to 2 per cent. of vanillin, the vanillin crystals are at least forty to fifty times as strong, and the employment of vanillin is, therefore, very much more economical and allows of introducing the flavor into the products, where the cost of the bean would be prohibitive. In flavoring peppermint, one does not use an extract of the herb, but a few drops of the volatile oil, although an extract of the herb would undoubtedly possess a slightly different flavor to that of the oil itself. The vegetable extractive of the peppermint herb would, however, not be appreciable in the finished product, and just as the oil of peppermint represents the flavoring principle of the herb, so does vanillin that of the vanilla bean. To appreciate thoroughly the triumph of synthetic chemistry in the production of vanillin, it should be borne in mind that it is chemically identical with the natural vanillin in the bean.

VANILLA SUBSTITUTE

A very good substitute for vanilla extract is made from vanillin, etc., and is as follows:

1 oz. vanillin	$0 75
6 pts. alcohol	1 92

5 pts. water ....
1 pt. syrup   06
1 oz. caramel color   02

The above formula is very good for ice cream and other cold work. Simply dissolve in diluted alcohol, then color with caramel and sweeten with sugar.

VANILLA SUBSTITUTE

1 oz. vanillin, cost, about....................... $0 75
1 lb. granulated sugar, dissolved in warm water....   06
Dissolve the vanillin in pint of the finest grain alcohol, at say....................................   32
Add the syrup of sugar and color with a little caramel...   02

                                              $1 15

Add sufficient water to make one gallon. This will give a fine flavor for ice cream. It would please some better if it contained two or three pints of alcohol instead of one, but this would add to the cost of the extract without really adding to its value. One large ice cream manufacturer is using this formula exclusively in quantities of two ounces to each ten-gallon batch of ice cream.

TRUE VANILLA

To make a true vanilla from vanillin, use the following:
1 oz. vanillin $0 75
1 pt. alcohol   35

1 oz. caramel $0 01
Add water to make one gallon..................... ....
1 lb. sugar 06

You can't do much better than this for ice cream. To make it more expensive, and so as to take a fancy of one who thinks he is an expert in flavors, use one pint of tincture of vanilla bean to the gallon, cost, say fifty cents a pint, but for all practical purposes it does not increase its value very much. Or you may use two pints or three pints if you like. If you want to make a vanilla without an artificial color use still more, say one-half gallon, or 50 per cent. of vanilla tincture from bean.

––––––

A $1.80 VANILLA EXTRACT

1 oz. vanillin $0 75
1 pt. alcohol 35
1 lb. sugar 06
1 pt. good tincture or first infusion of vanilla bean,
    color with caramel.......................... 69

Add water to make one gallon.

In the above you will have a very practical formula used quite extensively.

––––––

A SIXTY-CENT VANILLA EXTRACT

2 ozs. vanillin $1 50
1 oz. cumarin 30
1 gal. syrup of sugar, white..................... 50
1 gal. alcohol 2 50

Add water enough to make eight gallons. Color with caramel. This will cost you sixty cents per gallon and will make a good standard extract. If vanilla is not strong enough, add a little more cumarin.

BAKER'S VANILLA EXTRACT
(Eighty Cents Per Gallon)

1 oz. vanillin	$0 75
2 oz. cumarin	60
3 oz. benzoic acid	25
6 pts. alcohol	1 92
6 pts. glycerine	1 20
Caramel color	05
Water to make six gallons.........................	....

$4 77

This will cost eighty cents per gallon. The six pints of glycerine could be replaced with six pounds of sugar, still reducing the cost. Some eight or ten years ago a New York house made vanilla by the above formula and sold it in large quantities for twelve dollars per gallon. One of the largest houses in Chicago is now making it under the name of Baker's Vanilla and sells it at prices varying from five to six dollars per gallon.

FANCY VANILLA EXTRACT AT $3.11

Cut up the beans in a chopping bowl (some use a sausage grinder); pour on water first; then, after a few hours, not more than twenty-four hours at the longest, pour on alcohol;

let it stand, with occasional stirring, for at least four or five days; filter off; then add sugar in the form of a nice clear white syrup; add water enough to make at least two gallons, costing three dollars and eleven cents per gallon. The quantities are as follows:

1 lb. bourbon cuts $3 60
2 lbs. granulated sugar.......................... 12
1 gal. alcohol 2 50
1 gal. water ....

This mixture will not be as strong a flavor to please the majority of the people for ice cream purposes, but it is absolutely pure. However, you may add about one ounce of vanillin and a small amount of caramel if so desired.

LEMON EXTRACT No. 1

¾ lb. oil lemon (fresh; use no old oil at any price).
¼ oz. terpenless oil (genuine only).
8 oz. glycerine.
7 pts. alcohol (188 per cent.).
Few drops of yellow color.

The terpenless oil may be omitted, and one-half or four ounces of glycerine may be replaced by. four ounces soft water. Extract made according to the above formula needs no treatment except filtering. You may let stand a few days and then decant it. But then it is best to filter; the expense is trifling.

LEMON EXTRACT No. 2

7 ozs. oil lemon	$0 35
6 pts. alcohol	1 88
Magnesia and sugar	04

Cost to make, per gallon.................... $2 27

Pour the oil of lemon into a medium-sized wedgewood mortar; add two or three ounces granulated sugar and one-half ounce to one ounce powdered carbonate of magnesia, or put in enough magnesia to make mixture about as thick as molasses; then rub for three-quarters of an hour to one hour; this makes the oil more soluble so that more water can be used; now pour on the alcohol or put oil, etc., into a large bottle or other suitable receptacle and add the alcohol; shake, and then add hot (not boiling) water and color with a few drops of lemon yellow dissolved in alcohol or water. Some manufacturers use tincture of tumeric for coloring. Water enough should be added to yield one gallon extract after filtration. This will require about thirty-six ounces.

LEMON EXTRACT No. 3

2 oz. oil lemon	$0 10
½ gal. alcohol (188 per cent.)	1 25
Magnesia and sugar	04

Cost to make, per gallon.................... $1 39

Treat as in Formula No. 2, adding hot water to make one gallon.

LEMON EXTRACT No. 4

```
1 oz. oil lemon................................. $0 05
1 qt. alcohol .................................      63
Magnesia and sugar...........................      04
                                                 _____
    Cost to make, per gallon.................... $0 72
```

Add hot water to make one gallon. This will require to be very thoroughly rubbed in order to filter clear. This formula might be varied by using one-half ounce of oil and one-eighth ounce artificial citral; it will be easier to filter if so made.

LEMON EXTRACT No. 5

8 oz. oil lemon, 40 cents.
8 oz. water.
Alcohol to make one gallon.
2 drams tincture tumeric.
Proceed as Formula No. 1.
To make tincture tumeric, take as follows:
4 oz. powdered tumeric.
1 pt. alcohol.
Macerate for one week and filter.

LEMON EXTRACT TO COST $2.50

The following formula will make a very fine lemon extract, and is being put out by a large western house at about eight dollars per gallon:

6½ oz. oil lemon.
½ gal. alcohol (188 per cent.).
Magnesia and sugar.

Rub the oil in mortar with two tablespoonfuls of sugar and some magnesia for twenty to thirty minutes; pour on alcohol; let stand twenty-four hours and filter. I should have said that the water should be added gradually and, if quite warm or even hot, but not boiling, all the better; you had better add twenty ounces of water to allow for what is absorbed by the filter paper and lost by evaporation. About one fluid dram of lemon yellow color will be sufficient to color one gallon. In using color be careful not to use too much. The extract should be thoroughly shaken up and the magnesia and sugar distributed before you pour your extract from the filter. After you have filtered this lemon and got your full gallon of extract, you may wash the filter; that is to say, let about a quart of clear water run through it and keep this filtrate to be used as so much in making your cheap lemon. If you put about a tablespoonful of bone black (animal charcoal) into your filter it will clear it when it would not come clear without it. Six and one-half ounces to the gallon, or six and four-tenths ounces would be the exact amount of oil of lemon in order to make a 5 per cent. extract so as to pass in some food-law States. About seven ounces ought to be put in, as some is lost in filtration and by evaporation and in the analytical process itself.

A lemon about as good as the above for practical flavoring purposes, and better for soda fountains, may be made as follows:

3¼ oz. oil lemon $0 15
1½ drams true citral from lemon peel 23
5 pts. alcohol 1 60
Magnesia, etc., about. 03

This will cost two dollars per gallon, but this will not go into food-law States where 5 per cent. oil is required. All States do not require 5 per cent. Use water in the above formula as directed in other formulas.

ORANGE EXTRACT

Orange extract may be made in the same manner as directed for lemon. I think you may use a little less oil than in making lemon, and perhaps a little more alcohol. Color with orange color, or you may use one ounce tincture tumeric and perhaps just a trifle of caramel. A good many manufacturers use only the tincture of tumeric for coloring orange.

CITRIC ACID SOLUTION

Citric acid solution is made by dissolving one pound of citric acid in crystals, or in powdered form, into about one quart of water. Always place into glass bottle or glass jar.

ROOT BEER EXTRACT

1 pt. fluid extract of sarsaparilla.
2 ozs. fluid extract calamus.
4 fluid drams oil sassafras.
1 fluid dram oil wintergreen.
1 fluid dram oil anise.
1 pt. alcohol.
Caramel to color.
Water to make one gallon.

Mix the caramel with two pints water; add the fluid extracts, then the oil previously mixed with the alcohol, and finally enough water to make one gallon.

ROOT BEER EXTRACT No. 2

12 ozs. tincture of ginger.
12 ozs. extract of vanilla.
4 ozs. oil of sassafras.
2 ozs. oil of wintergreen.
1 oz. oil of anise.
¼ oz. oil of orange.
¼ oz. oil of cloves.
2 qts. alcohol.
3½ gals. simple syrup.
4 ozs. tincture of soap bark.
1 dram salicylic acid.
1¼ gals. caramel.

Water to make up six gallons; dissolve the oils and the salicylic acid in the alcohol; mix the syrup, water and caramel and add the other ingredients.

BIRCH BEER EXTRACT

4 parts sassafras.
2 parts wild cherry bark.
4 parts pimento.
4 parts wintergreen.
1 part hops.
2 parts coriander seed.

Percolate with dilute alcohol until forty parts of tincture are made.

INDEX

INDEX

INDEX

15